TALKS ON

American Law

TALKS ON
American Law

A SERIES OF BROADCASTS

TO FOREIGN AUDIENCES

BY MEMBERS OF

THE HARVARD LAW SCHOOL FACULTY

EDITED BY

Harold J. Berman

VINTAGE BOOKS

A DIVISION OF RANDOM HOUSE

NEW YORK

FOREWORD

In 1959 the United States Information Agency requested me to arrange a series of talks on American law to be broadcast in English to many countries of Europe, Asia and Africa by the Voice of America. The purpose of the broadcasts was to explain and discuss some of the basic characteristics of the American legal system; the talks were to be serious and scholarly, yet the speakers would have to bear in mind that most of the listeners would not only be non-lawyers but also strangers to America.

I agreed, on two conditions—which were granted. First, that there should be no censorship whatsoever, regardless of how critical of American law any of the speakers might be; second, that I might select all the speakers from among my colleagues on the Harvard Law School faculty. The reason for the first condition is obvious: scholarship and propaganda do not mix. The chief reason for the second condition was that administratively it would be much easier to coordinate the series if all participants were in one place. (Of course, Harvard Law School itself is in no way responsible for the series; the sixteen members of its faculty who have contributed talks have done so as individuals, and certainly the other thirty or so members of its faculty are not bound by any of our sins of omission or commission.)

The broadcasts were made over a period of several months in 1960, and elicited a very considerable interest among people in many countries throughout the world. Many requests for copies of the individual talks were received. When, however, the suggestion was made that the series be published in book form for American audiences, the speakers had some qualms. The talks had been prepared for foreigners; they were designed for oral presentation; they were very short, and made no pretense of being complete or systematic. Nevertheless, we decided to risk publication provided that it would be made clear to the American reader just what he is getting—which is not an "Introduction to American Law" or a "Critique of American Law," but a series of talks, seventeen in number, each approximately twenty-seven minutes in length, designed to explain to foreigners various aspects of the American legal system and to convey to them something of its purposes, its methods, its concepts and its spirit.

If the limitations of what is here presented are borne in mind, they may turn out to be not limitations at all but advantages. Simplification, repetition, concentration on a few points, explanation of what many might consider self-evident—these are not necessarily vices in a book about law for laymen. Even a certain defensiveness, which inevitably creeps into any attempt to portray one's native institutions to people of other countries, has some virtue here, for unfortunately, most Americans are "foreigners" to our own legal system and need to have it explained to them sympathetically.

Certainly, however, much is missing from these talks that would have been in them had they been prepared originally for American audiences. An example is furnished by the talk on Labor Law, in which the speaker chose to stress the nature of labor unions and the philosophy of collective bargaining—and consequently to omit many of the specific problems which are currently causing grief—for the very reason that labor unions play a quite different role and collective bargaining has a quite different rationale in most other countries. Indeed, in all the talks, which were severely limited by time, the choice of what the speakers emphasized was based, in part, upon the character of the audience.

Finally, a word of explanation is in order concerning the topics chosen for the individual talks. An attempt was made to achieve a fairly broad coverage of the American legal system. Yet the table of contents seems to reveal some glaring omissions. Where is federalism? Where is taxation? Where is trade regulation? They are touched upon in other chapters. Indeed, federalism comes up in almost every talk, which in itself shows how pervasive is its influence upon our law. Taxation and trade regulation are dealt with briefly in four of the talks. If the series had been longer, these three topics could have received separate discussion. Also some important aspects of our law which are omitted from the series altogether, such as family law and criminology, might well have been included.

Despite the inherent limitations of the form of presentation, we hope that this book will encourage some Americans who are laymen in the law to think deeply about our legal system. We hope also that some lawyers who already know everything that is contained in these pages will be stimulated by them to consider how *they* would portray the complex phenomena of our law to the vast numbers of otherwise educated people for whom it is either foolishness or a stumbling-block. For surely, one of the most important educational tasks of this generation is to overcome the widespread ignorance and mistrust of law, which plagues our scholarship in many fields and affects adversely our entire social order.

HAROLD J. BERMAN

Cambridge, Mass.
November 15, 1960

CONTENTS

TALKS ON

American Law

I

Harold J. Berman

THE HISTORICAL
BACKGROUND
OF AMERICAN LAW

IT IS DIFFICULT to capture the spirit of a legal system in seventeen short lectures. Law is, by nature, complex and technical—so much so that many people tend to view it with impatience and often even with cynicism. Yet law is one of the deepest concerns of all civilized men everywhere, for it offers protection against tyranny on the one hand, and anarchy on the other; it is one of society's chief instruments for preserving both freedom and order from arbitrary interferences by individuals, by classes, or by government itself. A portrayal of American law must therefore reflect American conceptions of freedom, of order, and of arbitrariness; yet such a portrayal must not oversimplify the intricate network of rules and procedures in which these conceptions are contained.

The purpose of this initial lecture is to offer a perspective for viewing American law as a whole—a perspective which may help the listener to understand the interrelationships of the various parts to be discussed separately in the succeeding lectures. I have chosen to cast that perspective in historical terms, in the belief that the continuity of our legal system in time, and its capacity for organic growth, reveal its fundamental qualities.

American law, viewed historically, is part of the family of Western legal systems. Its main institutional and doctrinal foundations were laid in the late eleventh and twelfth centuries in the monasteries and universities and in the ecclesiastical and royal households of Western Christendom. The jurists of that era transformed the primitive Germanic and Frankish legal systems through the inspiration of Roman law, of Greek philosophy, and of Hebrew and Christian ethics. Ultimately, diverse types of legal systems were built on these common foundations, but it is important to recognize that, as the English statesman Edmund Burke said two hundred years ago, "the law of every country of Europe is derived from the same sources."

The immediate parent of American law is English law, which the English colonists brought with them to the New World in the seventeenth and eighteenth centuries and which was formally "received" after the American Revolution by the various states of the Union as a foundation for their own law. Through this reception of English law the continuity of American law with the common Western legal heritage was preserved.

Thus it can be said that the American legal system was founded by King Henry II, who ruled England and Normandy in the last half of the twelfth century. It was Henry II who established in England, alongside the existing ecclesiastical legal system, the first permanent central law court, with professional judges and with a rational system of procedure. The decisions of the royal judges and the books written on the English common law in the twelfth and thirteenth centuries by no means describe American law as it exists today; nevertheless they reflect legal concepts and legal procedures which still have vitality.

Let me give an example. An important branch of American law is the law of torts. The word "tort" is Norman-French for "wrong," and the law of torts governs the remedies which one has against another who has wrongfully inflicted an injury upon his person or his property. Thus if a man intentionally strikes another, the victim may sue his assailant for compensation for the harm caused by the blow. Such a suit is called "an action for assault and battery"; it is a civil suit which must be tried separately from any criminal prosecution. The civil action, like the criminal action, will be tried by a jury of twelve laymen under the direction of a professional judge.

Now every one of the propositions which I have just stated concerning American law today may be traced directly to Bracton's treatise on English law, written in about 1250, and to still earlier decisions of the King's courts.

On the other hand, Bracton's treatise contains nothing about another type of tort, the "action for negligence," which offers a remedy to one who is injured by another, not intentionally, but carelessly. In 1250 the English "common" law—that is, the law common to the entire country, applied by the central courts— was not sufficiently developed to regulate injuries caused by negligence; indeed, it had taken a long step forward in providing a distinct civil remedy for harm caused by intentional acts of violence. If, however, one traces the history of English and American law through the centuries, one finds that the "action for negligence" was gradually developed by the courts on the analogy of the older "action for assault and battery." Both types of remedies grew out of the medieval English concept of "trespass"—a Norman-French word for the Latin "transgressio"—and out of the medieval English procedure which permitted a person who was a victim of a "trespass" to go to the King's Chancellor to procure a written order requiring the defendant to appear in the King's Court to answer the plaintiff's charge that he had committed the particular type of trespass alleged. Both the concept of trespass and the system of "writs" issued by the Chancellor classifying the plaintiff's charge were distinctive English adaptations of basic legal concepts and procedures developed throughout Western Christendom.

Another English adaptation of medieval Western legal ideas and procedures was the development by the Chancellor of special rules and procedures called "equity." In the fourteenth and fifteenth centuries the king's courts became rigid and narrow in their interpretation of their own functions and their own rules. The Chancellor, who next to the King was the most important official in the country, then set up a special office to hear grievances which the King's regular courts could not or would not handle adequately. The jurisdiction of the Court of Chancery, as this office came to be called, was said to be a matter "of conscience" or "of equity," and in time the term "equity" acquired a technical meaning, referring to the rules and procedures developed by the Court of Chancery, as contrasted with the rules and procedures of the courts of "common law." Equity procedure was more flexible than common-law procedure. In addition, suits in equity were not tried before a jury. Moreover, unlike the common-law courts, which in general would only award money compensation as a remedy, the Court of Chancery could order a party to do or not to do certain acts, and could punish him for contempt of court if he failed to obey. It could adjust its decrees to all the circumstances of the case. Moreover, chancery—or equity— enforced types of promises and arrangements which the common-law courts did not recognize; the most important of these was the so-called trust, under which a person transferred property to another to be held "in trust" for the benefit of a third person. Thus equity became a supplementary system of justice. The chancery court did not have a general jurisdiction over all kinds of disputes; it acted—and equity continues to act—

7

only in those cases where the remedy at common law is inadequate.

This dual system of courts of equity and courts of common law continued to exist and was carried over to the American colonies. In the nineteenth century, both in England and in the United States, there took place a merger, whereby the courts of chancery were generally abolished and the same judges administered both "law" and "equity." Yet in the minds of lawyers and judges the two systems are kept distinct. Certain remedies—such as a so-called injunction ordering a person to do or refrain from doing certain acts—are called "equitable remedies"; and rules of equity—that is, rules developed in the courts of chancery before their abolition—are applied to it. Similarly a "trust" is enforceable under equity rules.

Thus certain features which distinguish English and American law today from most other legal systems in the world must be explained in historical terms, and particularly in terms of the fact that English law, which was the most highly advanced of the secular legal systems of the Middle Ages, has preserved its continuity, despite many changes, both in England and in America.

The examples which I have already cited illustrate the medieval origins of the Anglo-American practice of trying all civil and criminal cases separately (in most legal systems the victim of a crime may bring his suit for money compensation as part of the criminal proceedings instituted by the state); of the Anglo-American practice of trial by jury in civil cases other than cases in equity (in most legal systems jury trial is generally confined to criminal cases); of the Anglo-American practice of classifying civil wrongs according to certain types which have been developed over the centuries by the courts, such as "assault and battery" and "negligence," to which could be added "trespass to land," "fraud," "slander," and many others (in most legal systems there are analogous types of wrongs, but they are generally defined by the legislature in a Civil Code rather than developed historically by judicial decisions); and of the Anglo-American concept of the "trust," which has become one of our most important devices not only for transfers of property on death but also for enforcing many types of business arrangements in which one person—for example, a director of a corporation—has the obligations of a trustee acting for the benefit of others (most legal systems contain no all-embracing principle corresponding to that of the Anglo-American trust, though they do contain various concepts which fulfill some of its functions).

The progress of English law in the Middle Ages was due in part to the early centralization of political and legal authority in the hands of the King. It was due also to the early development in England of a secular legal profession, with its own independent organization and its own traditions. Formed in the fourteenth century as a medieval guild, the English lawyers were members of fraternal societies called Inns of Court, where they trained their apprentices. Moreover the judges were and still are, both in England and America, generally appointed from among those who achieved distinction as practicing lawyers.

With the rise of strong monarchies throughout Europe in the sixteenth century, there was great pressure in all Western countries for a return to classical Roman law. In England, however, the medieval law had become well enough established as a national law, the secular legal profession was strong enough, the secular judiciary was sufficiently able, and, in general, the existing legal system was sufficiently rational and flexible, so that a radical legal transformation such as took place in the German, French and other principalities and kingdoms was not necessary or possible.

The English monarchs of the sixteenth and early seventeenth centuries were able to dominate the courts, and especially the courts of equity, in cases involving political matters; at the same time they created special courts with extraordinary powers, which, like the courts of equity, competed with the courts of common law. In the seventeenth century battle for parliamentary supremacy over the King, an important part of the judiciary and the legal profession were on the side of the Parliament, and leading judges openly reaffirmed the medieval principle that the King is under the Law, not above it. With the final triumph of Parliament, the King's special courts were dissolved and the judiciary, which previously had held office at the pleasure of the King, was granted independence and life tenure.

Thus the English who colonized America in the

seventeenth and eighteenth centuries brought with them the Western concept of the supremacy of law, as embodied in the English historical tradition. Yet much of the seventeenth-century English law was ill-adapted to conditions in the New World. Many of the privileges of the landed gentry were out of place in the frontier settlements; moreover, stability of family ties and of property relations was less important in the wilderness than equality of opportunity. Fortunately, English legal doctrine itself provided that the colonists carried with them only such laws of the mother country as were suitable to their new conditions. It was therefore possible for colonial courts and legislatures to make certain adaptations: in the law of inheritance, for example, to permit all children to inherit the land and not merely the oldest son as under the English rule of primogeniture; or in tort law, for example, to change the English rule that it was the duty of the owner of cattle to fence them in, a rule which made no sense on our wide-open frontier. Thus American law from the beginning was characterized by judicial and legislative creativity.

But the mother country refused to grant to the colonists all the legal rights of Englishmen. It was this more than any other single fact which ultimately caused the revolt against British rule. The American Declaration of Independence of 1776 consists chiefly of a list of charges of tyrannical abuses on the part of King George III, deprivations which the King was legally empowered to inflict upon his subjects in the colonies, although not upon his subjects at home. Thus the colonists charged that the King suspended laws passed by the colonial legislatures, made colonial judges dependent upon his will alone for their tenure, made the military superior to the civilian authority, refused to permit representation of the colonies in Parliament, and deprived the colonists, in many cases, of the benefits of trial by jury. The American Revolution was, in part, a secession of the colonies from England in order to enable the colonists to enjoy the rights of "free Englishmen."

Yet the American Revolution did not result simply in the establishment of the English system of government in America. Democratic ideas, opposed to the aristocratic and monarchical features of the English system, favored greater political equality, wider representation of the people in the state and national legislatures, greater local autonomy, and more freedom of the individual from governmental control. Public opinion, the goddess of the French Enlightenment, competed in America with the more conservative English traditions. Ultimately the United States achieved its own unique form of political system, which reflects a compromise between English and French ideas.

An important part of that compromise was the reception of the English common law—that is, of the rules laid down by English courts prior to the American Revolution—together with certain English statutes. For the original thirteen states on the Atlantic seaboard, this meant a continuation of their colonial legal institutions and doctrines; as new states were formed in the westward march across the American continent, it was generally provided in their Constitutions that the English common law, as it then existed, should form the basis of judicial proceedings.

In the first seventy-five years of our history as a nation, American judges, jurists, and legislators were able to develop out of the received English law a body of legal institutions and doctrines which reflected the social life of the new American polity—an *American* law. Let me try to state briefly some of the principal characteristics of this new American law which have persisted from the eighteenth and early nineteenth centuries to the present day.

We have seen that a significant feature of English law through the centuries has been the important role of the judiciary in the development of legal doctrine and, consequently, of the lawyers who frame the issues for judicial decisions. In the United States the role of the judiciary and of the legal profession has been still further enhanced. In part this is due to the existence of written federal and state constitutions, which set limits to the powers of the federal and state legislatures and specifically guarantee certain civil rights and liberties; constitutions whose interpretation, in the last analysis, is in the hands of the courts. In the nineteenth century the doctrine was developed in America that the courts can give no effect to any legislative or executive act which they find to be in violation of the federal or state constitutions.

Also the existence of a federal structure, in which the individual states have a great measure of independence, made it inevitable that the judiciary play a crucial role in maintaining the Constitutional balance between federal and state powers. Federalism, indeed, is one of the basic conditions of American law which has from the beginning influenced the development of all aspects of our system.

In addition, American law from the early nineteenth century on has been characterized by a higher degree of flexibility of judicial decision than English law in modern times. While accepting the English doctrine of precedent, whereby a court is bound to follow previous decisions of analogous cases, American courts have generally been more creative in reinterpreting earlier cases in order to adapt the law to changing conditions. Also American courts have not accepted the English doctrine that the highest court can never overrule its own precedents; the United States Supreme Court, as well as the Supreme Courts of the various states, have on occasion declared simply that one of their previous decisions was wrong and would not be followed.

Moreover, the American legal profession, although its historical roots are in the English Inns of Court which trained the leading American lawyers of colonial times, has developed its own characteristics. The apprenticeship system gradually gave way in the nineteenth century to university education in law; at the same time, the law faculty of an American university is constituted as a professional school, maintaining close connections with the practicing legal profession. Our lawyers have always been very numerous, and from their ranks have come a very large percentage of our presidents, congressmen, state governors, and other leading political figures, both national and local. Moreover, the continental dimensions of our country, and the diverse ethnic backgrounds of our people, have contributed to a tendency to turn to courts and to lawyers for the solution of the widest variety of economic, political, and social problems—problems which in many other countries are solved more informally by private business interests, by government officials, or by custom.

Finally, in the "formative era of American law" prior to the Civil War of 1861-1865, courts, lawyers, and legal scholars reshaped and modernized basic legal concepts of property, contract, corporations, negotiable instruments, and other areas of economic law. It would be wrong to suggest that the rules of law worked out in that era were "modern" in the sense that they would correspond to our needs today. Nevertheless, many of the basic concepts of our law were then freed from medieval survivals and put in a form which enabled them to be used more effectively by succeeding generations.

Thus many of the important features of the American legal system were established prior to the great industrial expansion which followed the Civil War. Of course, the enormous economic, political, and social changes of the past one hundred years have been accompanied by corresponding changes in our legal system. As we became a predominantly industrial and urban society, as the "big business" corporation emerged and labor organized, as communications developed to create a continental market and a continental culture, as our population doubled and quadrupled, our law inevitably became far more complex; and at the same time it became more systematized and more rationalized. Yet it is fair to say that most of our basic legal institutions and concepts antedate these vast changes; and further, that because of that fact, we have been able to assimilate change far more peacefully and efficiently than would otherwise have been possible.

If American law is viewed in the perspective of more than eight centuries, it is justifiable to lay stress on the creative role of the judiciary and of the legal profession, and on basic concepts of civil law and individual rights. In the perspective of more recent generations, the dominant factors seem to be legislative and administrative regulation of private activity. In the 1920's and 1930's, when the judiciary was often hostile to new social legislation, it became fashionable in many circles to advocate the emergence of the "administrative state," which would achieve "social justice" without the need for traditional legal procedures and categories. Yet time has shown that the judicial testing of statutory and administrative regulations by analogy of previous cases has a vital part to play not only in protecting individuals against abuse by officials but also in helping to make the official regulations themselves workable. Beyond this, there are values inherent in the judicial tradition and in the common law which can help us to anticipate and prevent the new barbarism of a technological age. Not the least of these values is that of tradition itself—that is, the vitality of historical experience as a starting point for solving the problems of the present and of the future.

II

John P. Dawson

THE FUNCTIONS
OF THE JUDGE

Visitors to our country find it strange that much of our law is found in reports of judicial decisions. We do not find this strange at all. It seems to us inescapable that judges should have a part in creating law—creating it as they apply it. In deciding the multifarious disputes that are brought before them, we believe that judges in any legal system inevitably adapt legal doctrines to new situations and thus give them new content. In our own system there is the further reason that our government is based on the fundamental premise that the power of government should be divided up among different groups which check and balance each other. In such a regime it seems both natural and wise that our judges should have a share of the power, with rules for its exercise.

Earlier court decisions from which law is derived are usually called "precedents." Literally this word merely means that the decisions were earlier, that they preceded. But our system is described as a system based on "precedent" because we consider that every judicial decision in some degree makes law for the future. We accept it so readily for several reasons, of which the first is simply historical.

English law, from which our law is derived, had from an early time been largely created by judges. The early settlers in this country, who were mostly English, were therefore familiar with this idea. But the new conditions of life on a great continent brought many problems in adapting English law to the American environment. In this process the judges necessarily played an important part. Furthermore, our written constitutions cast on our courts a great and new responsibility. Both the national government and the governments of each of our fifty states are created by constitutions that set limits to the governmental powers they confer. Included in these limits are constitutional guarantees to individuals, enforceable by them through appeal to the courts. Actions of the executive and even statutes passed by the legislatures will be declared wholly void if they infringe these basic guarantees. The net result is that the conditions of life in America and the governmental institutions we adopted have conferred on our judges powers and responsibilities that are more extensive than those known in England or indeed, I believe, in any other mature society in modern times.

But there is a second reason, which is at least as important as the historical factors I have described. Increasingly we have come to see the value of requiring our officials to give reasons for their decisions. The need is probably clearest in the case of judges, who are called on to adjudicate between the conflicting claims of individuals or groups. But a requirement that reasons be given is a safeguard as to other kinds of officials also. Though they may not seem completely convincing at the moment, when the reasons are understood they help to produce acceptance, they become part of a set of human purposes and they also give guidance for the future.

Even in the case of judges it has not always been so. In some countries in the past it has been thought that for judges to publish reasons would in some way undermine their authority. In England the judges from an early time engaged in free and informal argument with the lawyers who appeared before them. In this way the lawyers were given many clues as to the reasons why cases were decided as they were. The cases, with the reasons given, were reported by private reporters and studied by the legal profession for centuries. But it was not until late—in the nineteenth century—that it became established practice for the English judges, on their own responsibility, to write a full statement of reasons, in what we now call a judicial opinion. The same practice developed in France and Germany and other parts of western Europe at about the same time. We now consider it essential that the judges in our high appellate courts prepare and publish opinions, so that their reasons for decision will be open for everyone to inspect and to criticize. This is a job for the judges themselves, a function attached to their office. We regard this as so essential a safeguard against willful and arbitrary action, so important a restraint on the power of our public officials, that we have extended this requirement to administrative and other officials, wherever it is feasible.

The publication by judges of reasoned opinions, after the practice is once established, is apt to have further consequences. When decisions are known, especially if they are coupled with reasons, continuities are almost certain to develop. Surely Americans are not different from other human beings in wanting and expecting continuity and consistency in decisions, no matter who may make them. It is confusing and apt to seem unjust for the same problem to be decided in different ways merely because the decisions are made at different times or between different people. For the persons affected by decisions, consistency is an important virtue, not only because it permits prediction but because it seems more fair.

Our conception of judicial precedent is therefore in part a product of our own special history and is partly shaped by the modern practice of published court opinions, but it rests on a basic notion of fairness—that like cases should be decided alike. This is an idea that also seems valid for any legal system. Indeed, in legal practice there no longer seems to be an essential difference between Anglo-American law and the legal systems of western Europe, where the law is supposed to reside in Codes. In Western Europe—in fact, nowadays in most of the world—decisions of the highest courts are regularly published. And in Western Europe, at any rate, it appears that earlier cases are in fact followed, patterns of action do emerge.

Our theories about judicial precedent are often misunderstood by foreign critics, especially those trained in the use of codified systems of law. They think the theory of precedent enlarges unduly the powers of judges. But to us this does not seem true at all. Like the modern requirement that judges give reasoned opinions, compulsion to follow precedent is essentially a means of *limiting* power. It means that a court cannot decide the new case before it according to the impulse it may have at the moment, but must act consistently with prior decisions. It means that a past decision, whose reasons have been stated, must be followed in other similar cases to which the reasons apply, unless new and persuasive reasons can be found that dictate a different result. This seems to us another way of ensuring that power will not be arbitrary—one of the great objectives of any system that can properly be called a system of law.

It is true, of course, that both in theory and in our working techniques we lay more stress on judicial decisions than do countries outside the English tradition. We have a great quantity of law reports. The highest appellate courts regularly publish opinions in substantially all the cases that come before them. Many of the intermediate courts of appeal do likewise; even some trial-court opinions are reported, though this is on the whole rare. Opinions usually give a full statement of the facts, of the procedural history of the case, and then a quite elaborate discussion of the legal doctrines applicable. In this discussion prior decisions will almost always be referred to and their relevance to the current problem described. If the prior decisions are not considered relevant they will be distinguished. If they are found, for persuasive reasons, to have been wrongly decided, the prior decisions can be overruled, though on the whole this does not happen often. A judicial opinion in our practice is thus expected not only to give the reasons that are decisive in the particular case but to connect them up with the reasons given in analogous cases.

It is in this last respect, chiefly, that our practice differs from that of some other countries, such as France and Russia. But it does not differ in any essential way from the practice in some other countries with codified systems, such as Germany. This practice rests on the unspoken premise that it is part of the duty of the deciding court not only to expose its own reasons but, so far as time permits, to fit the case into a larger pattern. Our judges, in short, have a share in the task of keeping the law itself rational and self-consistent in the midst of new creation.

This conscious and explicit reliance on prior decisions brings many problems of analysis and requires use of some special techniques. The essential principle is that "like" cases should be decided alike. Then how does one determine what cases are "like"? Each case will differ somewhat from every other, if only in the names of the parties. The main clue must be found of course in the reasons given by the court itself for reaching the decision it did. But it often happens that sev-

J O H N   P.   D A W S O N

eral reasons are given, with differing degrees of general-
ity. When one projects back from a later case and ex-
amines these reasons, it may become clear that some
were broader than they needed to be. In such a case—
and this is a very common case—the reasons given that
are too broad can be disregarded. For judges are not
legislators. Not everything they say can be taken as
law. We do not read opinions as though they were
statutes. Primary responsibility for making new law
rests with the legislatures. The responsibility of judges
is to decide the cases, and only the cases, that are
brought before them. What judges say carries weight
and adds new content only to the extent that the reasons given are *necessary* to the decision of the case before them. And so we draw the distinction between the
holding (including the reasons necessary to explain the
result) and dicta (remarks or sayings that could have
been omitted without changing the result).

One might inquire: why not get rid of all these com-
plications and, where changes of law are needed,
simply rely on the legislatures? The members of the
legislatures are voted in or out of office because of the
action they have taken or promised to take on
the whole range of issues on which laws can be made.
Since they are elected for this purpose and directly responsible to the voters for the action they take or fail
to take, would it not be more democratic to rely on the
legislatures exclusively and deny that judges have any
law-making power whatever? One answer to this
question has already been given. There are constitutional limits to the powers, not only of the executive

but also of the legislatures. We have found no way of making these limits effective and of enforcing the guarantees they provide except to entrust their enforcement to our courts. This means that there are outside limits on what can be done, even by the legislatures. But the constitutions merely set outside limits. What about the problems that lie within those limits?

The fact is that we have a great many statutes. Thousands are passed each year, if one adds up the total production of the federal Congress and the legislatures of the fifty states. They cover a great variety of subjects— the powers and purposes of our public agencies, the very broad area of social welfare, and certain areas of private law, such as commercial law, in which we have resorted increasingly to small-scale codification. Many great changes in our society have been made by legislation, and it grows more important every year. In applying it our courts are required to recognize that the legislatures express, far more directly than judges can do, the needs and desires of the people. Where the intention of the legislature can be ascertained and constitutional limits are not exceeded, courts must defer to the legislative will and give effect to the legislature's decisions.

Why, then, not go further and express the whole body of law in comprehensive codes? We know this is the solution adopted in many countries of the world, in fact in most that lie outside the traditions of the English common law. There has been much discussion in this country of the virtues of codes. But on the whole the experience of countries with comprehensive codes has not encouraged us to move toward general codification. Human foresight cannot carry far enough, language and logic lack the resources, to provide in detail for all the enormous complexities of a great society. In western Europe, where the experience under codes has been longest and most fully recorded, the judges seem to act increasingly as our judges do, precedents are becoming increasingly important, and the creative nature of judges' work is more and more recognized. A purely deductive method, in which decisions are explained merely by citing some code provision, may seem to be simple, but it disguises the real choices that are inevitably involved. For large parts of our law, therefore, we will probably continue to rely on the methods of gradual change, case by case, as our experience unfolds.

If we must place so much faith in judges, the methods by which we select them become all the more important. In the federal courts and one-third of the states, the judges are named by the chief executive officer—the President of the United States or the governor of a state—often with a requirement that one house of the legislature concur. In two-thirds of our states the judges are elected by vote of the people. Whichever method is used, judges are chosen under different tests and are responsible for their performance in different ways than our other elected officials. We would not conceive that a judge should be expelled from office because he decided a case, or a series of cases, in a manner that a majority of the voters strongly disapproved, though this would probably happen to any other kind of elected official. In fact, in our federal system and in some of the states judges are appointed for life. It is more common for them to hold office for a fixed number of years—six, eight, or ten or perhaps even twelve. During the periods for which they are chosen, all judges are irremovable except for gross misconduct in office; and in our whole history the number of times that this has happened is extraordinarily few. In the states where the judges are elected by popular vote, most of them are re-elected and stability of tenure is achieved in fact.

Our judges, in short, are not mere civil servants. Most countries outside the tradition of the English common law have a career service for judges, with specialized training and promotion from within the service. We do not. With us, men and women come to be judges through successful work of other kinds—most of them as practicing lawyers. This means that most of them take office after they have reached mature life and after varied experience in the affairs of our society. For them, as for those who choose them, the office of judge is a most honorable one. To hold it, men are willing to sacrifice income and other advantages. Judges are prominent and respected persons in the communities they live in. This is true not only of the judges on the appellate courts, whose published opinions are the main source of the case-law I have just discussed. It is true also of the trial judges, who play a prominent and essential part in directing trials, ensuring impartial treatment of the litigants and their lawyers, guiding and instructing juries, and maintaining order and restraint in court-room procedure.

The use of juries in a large percentage of current litigation and the influence of jury trial in shaping our conceptions of trial procedure, have had the effect of restricting the role of trial judges, as compared with the role of trial judges in European procedure. Certainly in cases where juries are used, reliance on groups of laymen to make findings on disputed issues of fact makes the judge less dominant in the conduct of trials than he is apt to be in Europe. The complex adjustments that are produced by this division of functions will be discussed in later lectures in this series. But the trial judge, like the appellate judge, remains in our system a central figure. He is surrounded with much formality, for he is a symbol of neutrality and fairness. The formality expresses a widely held conviction that the impartial administration of justice, by independent judges, is an essential function of government in a civilized community.

Since judges are human beings with choices to make, not all of them measure up to our expectations. The use of popular elections in most of our states has led in some places to the choice of persons whose quality is mediocre or who are receptive to political influences. Even the appointive process is no guarantee that the ablest and most impartial will be chosen. After they assume office they are accountable only in indirect ways, and our ultimate reliance must be on the sense of honor and duty, the wisdom and self-restraint of the individual holders of judicial office. But in a tradition in which these qualities are highly honored, men and women can be found who possess them. There are few Americans who would say that on the whole our trust in judges is misplaced. The responsibilities cast on them are great, but no greater than they need to be in a vast and expanding democratic society, whose freedom is tempered by respect for law.

III

~~~~~~

Lon L. Fuller

THE ADVERSARY

SYSTEM

THE EXPRESSION "the adversary system" can be used in a narrow sense. When we speak of "the adversary system" in its narrow sense we are referring to a certain philosophy of adjudication, a conception of the way the trial of cases in courts of law should be conducted, a view of the roles that should be played by advocates and by judge and jury in the decision of a controversy.

The philosophy of adjudication that is expressed in "the adversary system" is, speaking generally, a philosophy that insists on keeping distinct the function of the advocate, on the one hand, from that of the judge, or of the judge from that of jury, on the other. The decision of the case is for the judge, or for the judge and jury. That decision must be as objective and as free from bias as it possibly can. The Constitution of Massachusetts provides—in language that in its idiom calls at once to mind the spirit of a great age, the Age of the Enlightenment and of the American and French Revolutions—that "It is the right of every citizen to be tried by judges as free, impartial and independent as the lot of humanity will admit." If the judge is to perform that high function—a function which the Constitution recognizes may put human nature to a severe test—then the rules of procedure that govern a trial must be such that they do not compel or invite him to depart from the difficult role in which he is cast. It is not his place to take sides. He must withhold judgment until all the evidence has been examined and all the arguments have been heard.

The judge and jury must, then, be excluded from any partisan role. At the same time, a fair trial requires that each side of the controversy be carefully considered and be given its full weight and value. But before a judge can gauge the full force of an argument, it must be presented to him with partisan zeal by one not subject to the restraints of judicial office. The judge cannot know how strong an argument is until he has heard it from the lips of one who has dedicated all the powers of his mind to its formulation.

This is the function of the advocate. His task is not to decide but to persuade. He is not expected to present the case in a colorless and detached manner, but in such a way that it will appear in that aspect most favorable to his client. He is not like a jeweler who slowly turns a diamond in the light so that each of its facets may in turn be fully revealed. Instead the advocate holds the jewel steadily, as it were, so as to throw into bold relief a single aspect of it. It is the task of the advocate to help the judge and jury to see the case as it appears to interested eyes, in the aspect it assumes when viewed from that corner of life into which fate has cast his client.

This is in general what we mean by the adversary system when we apply that phrase to the trial of controversies before courts. As I have indicated, there is a broader use of the phrase which extends it—by way of analogy and with many qualifications—to decisions not rendered by judges and juries but in the great society that lies outside the courtroom. There is a kind of adversary system that may be said to underlie the conduct of a legislative chamber, an industrial enterprise, or a university. I shall touch briefly on some aspects of this broader conception toward the end of my talk. For the time being I should like to examine more closely the adversary system which underlies the trial of cases in courts of law.

Let me begin with that aspect of the adversary philosophy which is most puzzling—not to say, most offensive—to the layman. The ethical standards of the legal profession make it perfectly proper for a lawyer to undertake in a criminal case the defense of a man whom he knows to be guilty.

It should be carefully noted that in the United States a lawyer is not bound to defend a guilty man. Unless he has been appointed by the court to act as a public defender, the lawyer may decline to defend a man with whom he does not wish to be associated, whether that man be guilty or innocent. The rule I am discussing is one which says that without impropriety a lawyer may, if he sees fit, defend a man he knows to be guilty. Not only that, but the lawyer may render this service for a fee; he may, without qualms of conscience, accept compensation for appearing in court to plead the cause of a man whom he knows to be guilty.

At this point the layman is apt to lose his patience with the legal profession and its curious moral views. "Surely," he says, "something must be wrong when, on the one hand, we have courts that are supposed to find out whether a man is actually guilty and when, on the other, we allow a skilled lawyer to come into court to help a guilty man with his persuasive skill. Since the whole object of the machinery of justice is to separate the guilty from the innocent, the lawyer ought to advance that object by coming forward and informing the court that his client is guilty." So the layman is likely to view the matter.

Nor is the layman often convinced by the arguments generally advanced to justify the lawyer in defending a man he knows to be guilty. What are those arguments? Well, it is said that a man charged with crime should not have his guilt determined in the privacy of a lawyer's office but in open court by due process of law. If every lawyer whom the accused approaches declines to take the case because he appears to be guilty, then the accused is, in effect, condemned out of court and denied the formal trial to which the law entitles him. It is further said that appearances are often deceiving; many a man has appeared to be plainly guilty until the patiently turning wheels of justice disclosed his innocence. Even confessions are not always to be trusted. Cases are not uncommon where a woman, let us say, confesses to a crime in order to save her guilty husband. Or again, a person under great mental stress and moved by some obscure desire for self-punishment may confess to a crime he never committed so that he may expiate imaginary ones. Because all these things can happen and inferences of guilt are so often mistaken, it is argued that the lawyer has no right to judge the guilt or innocence of his client before the case is tried. If he refuses to defend a client because he thinks he is guilty, the lawyer is wrongfully usurping the office of judge and jury.

How convincing to the layman is this attempt to justify the rule? I do not think it is likely to remove his doubts. The argument is apt to seem to him a little too clever, a little too pat. What then do I as a lawyer think of the argument? I think it has some validity. I reach this conclusion on the basis of the testimony of some of my brothers of the bar. A lawyer who has a wide experience in criminal cases can sometimes give a dramatic instance where he represented a client he firmly believed to be guilty only to have some unexpected turn in the evidence prove that his client was innocent.

Yet even this sort of experience is not wholly decisive of the issue. It may be answered that all human judgments are subject to error. One must calculate probabilities. We may concede that there is some chance that an experienced lawyer, with a knowledge of human nature and access to the most intimate facts, may erroneously conclude that his client is guilty when in fact he is innocent. But the chance is so slight that it may be argued it should be neglected in the actual conduct of affairs.

We may attempt to answer this argument in turn by saying that where the guilt or innocence of a human being is in issue, a calculation of mere probabilities is out of place. But the true answer goes deeper. The reason lies in considerations of an order different from those I have so far been discussing. The purpose of the rule is not merely to protect the innocent person against the possibility of an unjust conviction, precious as that objective is. The purpose of the rule is to preserve the integrity of society itself. It aims at keeping sound and wholesome the procedures by which society visits its condemnation on an erring member.

Why have courts and trials at all? Why bother with judges and juries, with pleas and counterpleas? When disputes arise or accusations are made, why should not the state simply appoint honest and intelligent men to make investigations? Why not let these men, after they have sifted the evidence and resolved apparent contradictions, make their findings without the aid of advocates and without the fanfare and publicity of a trial?

Arrangements tending in this direction are not unknown historically. One of them has at various times and in various forms been familiar on the European continent. This is the institution of the investigating magistrate, *le juge d'instruction, der Untersuchungsrichter*. In important criminal cases this official makes his own investigations and reaches his own conclusions on the basis of the evidence. To be sure, he has never been given the power to make a final determination of guilt. Yet his findings tend to influence the trial that follows; the form he has given to his inquiry tends to shape the proceedings in court and often tips the balance in cases of doubt.

No such office or institution exists in the countries of the common law, including the United States. Why do we reject an arrangement that seems so reasonable in its quiet efficiency? In answer I might simply draw on the European experience and quote a French observer who remarked that in cases where the *juge d'instruction* reaches the conclusion that no prosecution should be brought, it is usually with a tinge of regret that he signs the necessary documents. European experience also suggests that political interests are often involved in charges of crime and that it is desirable in order to prevent abuse that every fact bearing on guilt be tried in courts open to the public.

But publicity is not of itself a guarantee against the abuse of legal procedures. The public trials of alleged traitors that nearly always follow violent revolutions are a sufficient testimonial to this fact. What is essential is that the accused have at his side throughout a skilled lawyer, pledged to see that his rights are protected. When the matter comes for final trial in court, the only participation accorded to the accused in that trial lies in the opportunity to present proofs and reasoned arguments on his behalf. This opportunity cannot be meaningful unless the accused is represented by a professional advocate. If he is denied this representation the processes of public trial become suspect and tainted. It is for this reason that I say that the integrity of society itself demands that the accused be represented by counsel. If he is plainly guilty this representation may become in a sense symbolic. But the symbolism is of vital importance. It marks society's determination to keep unsoiled and beyond suspicion the procedures by which men are condemned for a violation of its laws.

The lawyer appearing on behalf of an accused person is not present in court merely to represent his client. He represents a vital interest of society itself, he plays an essential role in one of the fundamental processes of an ordered community. The rules that govern his conduct make this clear.

It is a fundamental principle of the lawyer's canons of ethics that he may not state to the judge or jury that he personally believes in the innocence of his client. He may say, for example, "I submit that the evidence fails to establish the guilt of my client." But he may not say, "I personally know my client to be innocent," just as he may not be asked by the judge or jury whether he believes his client to be guilty.

These rules concerning the lawyer's conduct in court are not only important in themselves, but also for the spirit that lies back of them. They make it clear that the lawyer is present, not as an individual with all of his likes and dislikes, beliefs and disbeliefs, but as one who plays an important role in the process of social decision. At no time is the lawyer a mere agent of his client. If he disapproves of his client's conduct during the trial, he may—though this is often a painfully difficult decision—withdraw from the case. Obviously, he may not participate in the fabrication of testimony, just as he may not, to free his client, cast suspicion on innocent persons.

So important is the defense lawyer's role that where the accused cannot find a lawyer who will represent him, or cannot afford to pay for a lawyer, it is the practice for the court to appoint a lawyer to represent him. Under our constitutional system a failure of the court to do this may render a conviction against the accused invalid. Notwithstanding these formal guarantees, our American practice at present leaves much room for improvement. The public service of defending a man, who would otherwise be without a lawyer, is usually poorly paid, and busy and able lawyers are often loath to take on the burdens of such an assignment. There is, however, an active movement now to improve this situation and to provide adequately paid and competent counsel for every person accused of serious crime.

I have so far emphasized chiefly the role of the lawyer in the defense of criminal cases. But the need for an adversary presentation, with both sides vigorously upheld, is also present in civil suits. For one thing, there is an element of social condemnation in almost all adverse legal judgments, so that the considerations that apply to criminal cases are also relevant to civil controversies. To be found guilty of negligent driving or of breaking a contract does not carry the stigma of a criminal conviction, but in these cases, too, society must be concerned that even the qualified condemnation implied in an adverse civil judgment should not be visited on one who has not had a chance to present his case fully.

More important in complicated controversies is the contribution that an adversary presentation makes to a properly grounded decision, a decision that takes account of all the facts and relevant rules. In a statement issued recently by a committee of the American Bar Association, it was pointed out how, in the absence of an adversary presentation, there is a strong tendency by any deciding official to reach a conclusion at an early stage and to adhere to that conclusion in the face of conflicting considerations later developed. In the language of the committee:

"What generally occurs in practice is that at some early point a familiar pattern will seem to emerge from the evidence; an accustomed label is waiting for the case and, without waiting further proofs, this label is promptly assigned to it. It is a mistake to suppose that this premature cataloguing must necessarily result from impatience, prejudice or mental sloth. Often it proceeds from a very understandable desire to bring the hearing into some order and coherence, for without some tentative theory of the case there is no standard of relevance by which testimony may be measured. But what starts as a preliminary diagnosis designed to direct the inquiry tends, quickly and imperceptibly, to become a fixed conclusion, as all that confirms the diagnosis makes a strong imprint on the mind, while all that runs counter to it is received with diverted attention.

"An adversary presentation seems the only effective means for combating this natural human tendency to judge too swiftly in terms of the familiar that which is not yet fully known. The arguments of counsel hold the case, as it were, in suspension between two opposing interpretations of it. While the proper classification of the case is thus kept unresolved, there is time to explore all of its peculiarities and nuances."

This phrasing of the matter makes it clear, I believe, why an adversary presentation of a controversy is perhaps the most effective means we have of combating the evils of bureaucracy. Bureaucracy exists, of course, in all countries, and it is a force for good as well as evil. But is it not true that whenever we use the term "bureaucrat" in a critical sense, we mean an official who, in the language I have quoted, tends "to judge too swiftly in terms of the familiar that which is not yet fully known," an official who concludes, before I have had a chance to explain my case to him, that it is just like that of the man who was ahead of me in the line? And is not the only sure cure for this evil an adversary presentation that will "hold the case . . . in suspension between . . . opposing interpretations," until the deciding official can "explore all its peculiarities and nuances"?

I do not have time to explore all the implications of the adversary system, nor to compare the different ways in which that system and its underlying philosophy find expression in the laws of different countries. I should like, however, to record my discontent with the implications sometimes drawn from the adversary system in my own country. One of these lies in the notion that a judge should throughout the trial remain passive; somewhat like a well-behaved child, he speaks only when spoken to. His role is thought of as being that of an umpire who is stirred to action only when he must resolve a dispute that arises between the contending lawyers. This notion is, I believe, based on a profound mistake. The essence of the adversary system is that each side is accorded a participation in the decision that is reached, a participation that takes the form of presenting proofs and arguments. If that participation is to be meaningful it must take place within an orderly frame, and it is the duty of the judge to see to it that the trial does not degenerate into a disorderly contest in which the essential issues are lost from view. Furthermore, when the party is given through his attorney an opportunity to present arguments, this opportunity loses its value if argument has to be directed into a vacuum. To argue his case effectively, the lawyer must have some idea of what is going on inside the judge's mind. A more active participation by the judge —assuming it stops short of a prejudgment of the case itself—can therefore enhance the meaning and effectiveness of an adversary presentation.

I have only a few minutes to touch on an expanded sense of the adversary system that applies its philosophy to decisions reached by less formal procedures, let us say, decisions reached in the course of operating an industrial or educational enterprise. In the conduct of any human enterprise, collective decisions must always involve a compromise of interests that are at least partially divergent. For example, in the operation of a factory one may distinguish among the following groups: (1) those whose primary objective is to produce a maximum of goods, (2) those whose primary interest is in developing a satisfied work force, working under conditions of complete dignity and impartial justice, and (3) those whose main urge is to improve the product, even at the cost of some present inefficiency. Each of these interests is a legitimate and proper one, yet each must be qualified by a recognition of the legitimate demands of the others.

An effective consensus cannot be reached unless each party understands fully the position of the others. This understanding cannot be obtained unless each party is permitted to state fully what its own interest is and to urge with partisan zeal the vital importance of that interest to the enterprise as a whole. At the same time, since an effective consensus requires an understanding and willing cooperation of all concerned, no party should so abandon himself in advocacy that he loses the power to comprehend sympathetically the views of those with different interests. What is required here is a spirit that can be called that of tolerant partisanship. This implies not only tolerance for opposing viewpoints, but tolerance for a partisan presentation of those viewpoints, since without that presentation they may easily be lost from sight.

A passage from John Stuart Mill is eloquent on this point: "We need not suppose that when power resides in an exclusive class, that class will knowingly and deliberately sacrifice the other classes to themselves: it suffices that, in the absence of its natural defenders, the interest of the excluded is always in danger of being overlooked; and, when looked at, is seen with very different eyes from those of the persons whom it directly concerns."

In the end, the justification for the adversary system lies in the fact that it is a means by which the capacities of the individual may be lifted to the point where he gains the power to view reality through eyes other than his own, where he is able to become as impartial, and as free from prejudice, as "the lot of humanity will admit."

IV

❯❯❯-❯❯❯-❯❯❯❮❮❮-❮❮❮-❮❮❮

Benjamin Kaplan

TRIAL BY JURY

IF WE ARE to be faithful to the purpose of this series
of lectures, to convey to you something of the shape
and color and spirit of the American legal system, then
we must speak of the jury. For this institution is not
only important in itself as a part of our court procedures; it has exerted a mighty influence upon other
elements of the court process. Like iron filings around
a magnet, many features of our law arrange themselves
around the jury.

What is the jury? In essence it is a group of citizens
—usually twelve in number—who perform particular
functions in the trial of a case, criminal or civil. Let me
say now that there is no such thing as "trial by jury" in
the sense of a case being heard by the jury alone, without the guidance of a professional judge. But while the
judge guides the jury, he may not attempt to overmas-
ter it or to usurp its functions. The relation between
judge and jury, as you will see, is best described as a

cooperative one in which each is to respect the other's independence.

I shall now describe very briefly the usual sequence in the trial of an action before judge and jury. First an array of men and women drawn from the qualified voters of the community is brought into court. This group is questioned by the judge and the lawyers on both sides in order to eliminate any individuals who have a connection with the litigants or who for some other reason may be biased. A jury is thus selected which is sworn to do justice and is seated in a jury box at right angles to the judge's bench. The trial proper then begins.

It is up to the lawyers acting for the litigants—the state and the accused in a criminal prosecution, the plaintiff and defendant in a civil action—to bring the evidence forward before judge and jury. Witnesses on one side, then on the other, are called and examined and cross-examined by the lawyers. The judge presides over this process but the initiative is with the litigating parties. If any evidence offered by one side is objected to by the other as being irrelevant or otherwise inadmissible under the rules of evidence, the judge decides then and there whether to admit or reject it. When the presentation of the evidence has been completed, the lawyers make partisan speeches in which they sum up the proof from their respective points of view.

Considered analytically, two all-important jobs now remain to be done, and here we must observe the relation between judge and jury. The first job is that of pronouncing the legal rules which are to govern the case. This is for the judge. The second job is to decide which version of the disputed evidence is true. This is for the jury. The two tasks are carried out as follows. The judge makes a speech to the jury, called a "charge," in which he states the applicable legal norms. He also rehearses the evidence, organizing it in logical fashion and indicating what are the crucial points of contradiction or doubt upon which the jury will have to pass. After hearing the charge, the jury withdraws from the courtroom, enters a separate chamber, and deliberates in secret upon the case. The judge may not go into the jury room, nor may he at any time during the trial make any private communication to the jury or to any individual juror. When the jury has reached a verdict —which typically must be by unanimous vote—it returns to the courtroom and announces it without explanation or justification: a verdict for the state or for the accused in a criminal case; for the plaintiff or for the defendant in a civil case, and if for the plaintiff, then a statement of the amount of damages to be paid. The verdict is to be understood as a short declaration by the jury that, having resolved the disputes of fact and having applied to the facts, as it has found them, the legal precepts received from the judge, the jury is satisfied that the party named in the verdict deserves to succeed.

And that is the end of the case in the court of first instance, subject to a certain limited power in the judge to set aside the jury's verdict if he is convinced that it was clearly unreasonable. When a verdict is thus set aside, the consequence often is that the case must be retried before a judge and another jury. But there is one kind of verdict which may not be set aside. That is a jury verdict acquitting the accused in a criminal case.

This extraordinary institution of the jury, by which laymen participate in a vital and decisive way in the administration of justice—how did it originate? We find here a curious adaptation of an ancient form to new uses. The Norman duke who crossed the English channel nearly nine hundred years ago was already acquainted with an administrative device for summoning a group of inhabitants to swear of their own knowledge about royal rights and privileges in the particular locality. A similar group of swearers—called juratores or jurors—began to be used by the royal judges in the twelfth century to declare certain rights in dispute between private parties. Jurors were also called on to "present" or accuse men of crimes committed in the neighborhood so that they might be brought to trial by the ordeal for judgment of guilt or innocence. When the Pope in the year 1215 forbade the clergy to lend religious sanction to the ordeal, the accused were induced—sometimes by torture—to accept the verdict of jurors on the ultimate question of their guilt.

In time, barbarism and magic were eliminated. Trial by jury became the chief method of trial both in the criminal and civil spheres in the royal courts, save only the so-called courts of equity which used a quite different procedure. Over the years the character of the jurors was transformed: they ceased to act as neighbors who decided according to their own knowledge of the case or on the basis of local rumor, and became, instead, neutral triers who were to decide solely on the basis of evidence produced in court. Still the jury was under a cloud, for the judges used to browbeat and punish jurors for bringing in verdicts not to the judges' liking. Especially was this a threat to personal liberty in prosecutions affecting the political interests of the Crown, for the judges sometimes identified themselves with the royal policy and pressed juries mercilessly for convictions. In part as a result of resistance by stalwart jurors, in part because the judges themselves achieved a sense of full independence from the King, the practice of threatening and punishing jurors disappeared, and the jury finally secured its freedom to decide as the right and justice of the cause might appear to it.

When the American colonies declared their freedom from Britain, the prestige of the jury as a guardian of the liberty of citizens was running very high. A right to trial by jury was written into the constitutions of the states and the Constitution of the United States. It remains in those constitutions today. And so the accused in a criminal prosecution for any but a petty offense, a party in a civil case other than one fitting into the old jurisdiction of a court of equity, is today entitled to demand jury trial as a matter of constitutional right. The trial of most serious criminal prosecutions today is by jury. Jury trial is also claimed in a considerable number of civil cases, although waiver of jury in such matters is common and is probably increasing in frequency. Where the jury right is not available or is not claimed, trial is by the judge alone, who decides not only the law but the facts.

Trial by jury continues to flourish in the United States. But are there rational grounds for the continued existence of this old institution? After all, our judiciary now holds equal and coordinate rank with the executive and legislative departments of government; it is not under suspicion of subservience to either of the other branches. Our judges are skilled professionals. Under modern conditions, with cases, especially civil cases, increasing in complexity, why should not the whole business of deciding cases be committed to the judges? Why should we continue to use the jury, an expensive and cumbersome piece of legal machinery?

For it must be admitted that trial by jury is expensive and cumbersome. Selection of juries can be a laborious process. Presentation of evidence to a group of laymen is necessarily more difficult and time-consuming than proof to a judge alone. Jury trial involves summing-up speeches by the lawyers and a charge by the judge; the former can be eliminated or at least shortened, the latter is entirely unnecessary in trial to a judge without a jury. With protraction of time and effort, jury trial results in higher costs, not only to the state, but to private parties engaged in litigation. It contributes to delay of civil cases on the court calendars. But apart from all this, can we really expect juries, untrained citizens ignorant of law, often of limited education, brought together to serve for a short time and unable to acquire experience in the arts of

49

judging—can we expect them to be a material help in the administration of justice? Will they not rather be easily misled into foolish verdicts by the strident advocacy of the lawyers?

Here it will be worthwhile, I think, to distinguish broadly between criminal and civil cases, and when we consider civil cases to make some further distinctions.

Jury trial on the criminal side means this: that before a man's life or freedom or reputation is taken from him by the state, his guilt, and the degree of it, must have been made manifest not merely to the professional mind but to the man on the street—or rather to twelve such men speaking with a single voice. Observe again that a verdict of acquittal is wholly immovable; a verdict of guilty may be undone if plainly unreasonable. There is, I think, ground to believe that the jury, operating on the whole as an additional procedural safeguard to the accused, and bringing lay judgment to the aid of the professional, does over the long run help to secure a satisfactory application of the criminal laws and, above all, to sustain public confidence in the process. In an extremity the jury would stand as a barrier to official persecution under the forms of law.

So much for the jury in criminal cases. In civil matters the question of the contribution of the jury is open to much greater doubt. Does the American style of jury have any proper place in the trial of commercial cases? To be sure, the highly complex or very technical commercial matters will generally fall into the equity classification where no right to trial by jury exists. But there are still many commercial cases to which the jury right does attach. Jury trial appears to have little advantage in those civil cases, not entirely confined to the commercial field, which cannot be thoroughly understood without some base of technical experience, and in which it is important that decision upon recurring fact-patterns shall be predictable and regular. It is in such cases, indeed, that jury trial is often waived by the parties.

Quite different considerations apply to large classes of civil cases where the legal rules themselves appeal to general community standards of justifiable and unjustifiable conduct as they exist at the particular time. Here it may well be that the blending interaction of judge and jury produces sounder average results than would the work of the judge alone, removed as the judge to some extent must be from the rough and tumble of life. It has been suggested, too, that there are certain kinds of disputes—for example, defamation actions and family quarrels—where the very anonymity of a jury verdict can have a salutary effect in putting embittered controversies really to rest.

Inexperienced triers are no doubt at an initial disadvantage in assessing and resolving conflicting testimony. The jury needs the judge's help in reducing the case to its essentials. When the judge provides this help, when he puts to the jury, fairly and clearly, the precise issues with which it has to deal, then the jury's consensus, its combined judgment of the credibility and reliability of witnesses, may be surer than the judge's own opinion. So, at any rate, judges have themselves often attested. A distinguished English judge

recently remarked that judges err on the side of thinking that all men are as logical as they are: juries tend
to make better allowance for the muddleheadedness
and blundering of simple people. In the end we must
recognize that fact-finding in courts of law is inevitably
an amorphous process, and it is hard to make exact
scientific tests of the accuracy of jurors—or, for that
matter, of the accuracy of judges.

Do juries really understand the legal rules pro-
nounced by the judges, which they are supposed to
take and apply to the facts? Much certainly depends
on the care and deliberation with which the judges
state the law for the benefit of juries. Where the legal
rules are irreducibly difficult, the device of a so-called
special verdict commends itself for use: the jury is asked
to respond only to a series of specific questions of
fact; the judge then applies the law to the answers
given by the jury and himself enters judgment for
plaintiff or defendant. Special verdicts have had some
vogue in civil cases in this country and should perhaps
be employed more often than they have been.

Juries are sometimes criticized for refusing to apply
the law as given by the judges, for inventing their own
law. A verdict may indeed mask or conceal a deviation
from the legal rules as laid down by the judge. Deliber-
ate refusal of juries to follow the judge's charge is probably infrequent; subtle, unconscious disregard may occur more often. Consider the automobile accident
cases which appear in very large numbers on our civil
calendars. According to the strict law, liability turns
on proven fault, on negligence. We may surmise that

a jury will react strongly to the plight of an injured plaintiff, and when the jury has reason to think that a defendant can afford to pay or is covered by insurance —matters which in strictness the jury should not consider—it may find for the plaintiff, even if proof of the defendant's negligence is notably weak. But when the jury appears in this somewhat lawless role it is time to inquire whether the law does not need revision. In fact our legal science has become doubtful of the fairness of some of the rules that are now nominally applied to these traffic-accident cases. We are thus reminded that in its long history the jury has on occasion been a leavener of the strict law, a kind of critic and irregular reformer of the law, anticipating formal legal change.

We have been examining, briefly and superficially, the contributions of the jury, positive and negative, to the handling of particular kinds of litigation. But we ought to acknowledge that jury trial is more than the sum of these plus and minus factors. On the one hand, jury service can teach some understanding of the awesome difficulties of judging, some respect for the judicial qualities of dispassion and restraint. On the other hand, judges required to work with jurors day in and day out are unlikely to develop the law as a mysterious abstraction divorced from life. In another sense the jury embodies the insight that the administration of justice is too important to be left altogether to the professionals.

I said at the outset that the jury had put its impress on our whole court process. I pass over particular legal doctrines developed in response to the jury—for example, rules on admission and rejection of evidence. The larger fact is that jury trial must be carried out as a single continuous episode and in such a manner as to convey meaning to a group of ordinary listeners; for the jury cannot be dismissed and reconvened over a period of time and it must receive its impressions largely by ear. The resulting concentration and orality of jury trial lend a high dramatic quality even to our ordinary litigation; and these characteristics have extended themselves to trial before the judge alone. But if trial is concentrated, if it is to take place without opportunity for *arrière-pensées*, then the opposing sides must appear in court fully prepared. This means vigorous work by the contending lawyers in preparation for trial, which in turn enables them to be vigorous in contention at the trial. And so jury trial has profoundly affected the character of the legal profession.

But here I trespass on other subjects in this lecture series, the adversary system and the role of lawyers in our society, and I must bring my remarks to a close.

V

Livingston Hall

THE RIGHTS
OF THE ACCUSED
IN CRIMINAL CASES

As I START this talk, I hold in my hands a 440-page book entitled *Sources of Our Liberties*. More than seven hundred fifty years of Anglo-American custom, traditions and law are summarized in this collection of thirty-two documents and commentaries. Starting with Magna Carta—the Great Charter of 1215 in England—these are the instruments through which there came into existence in England and America "established and known rules of law limiting the authority and discretion of men wielding the power of government."

These documents—ending with the Twenty-Second Amendment to the United States Constitution adopted in 1951—confirm and witness an infusion of moral principles into Anglo-American legal institutions. Nowhere has this been more clearly evident than in the growth of the rights of the accused in criminal cases.

The guarantee of the 39th Article of Magna Carta provided that no freeman should be imprisoned, dispossessed, banished or destroyed "except by the legal judgment of his peers or by the law of the land." This was extended in the fourteenth century to provide that "no man of what estate or condition that he be, shall be . . . taken nor imprisoned . . . nor put to death, without being brought in answer by due process of law." When the English first came to settle America, these rights in criminal cases were carried with them, in the First Charter of Virginia of 1706, granted to them by King James I.

It would be a mistake, however, to believe that the right to "due process of law" granted to accused persons is primarily their own personal privilege. On the contrary, "due process of law" represents a pledge to the entire community that our police, our prosecuting officials and our courts will behave properly toward us all, in obedience to rules of law which have grown out of centuries of experience.

The mere existence of rights does not automatically guarantee that they will always be honored. Our law reports record a number of instances in which courts have had to act to correct abuses of power by overzealous public officials. Criminal surveys have also focused attention on specific areas (such as wire tapping) in which illegal methods have proved particularly difficult to eradicate.

It is important to know how far the rights of our individuals are enforceable. Do there exist effective ways for the correction of errors in our criminal proceedings? Before attempting to answer this final question, however, it appears desirable to describe in greater detail the specific rights now granted to accused persons by the still-developing rules of law which govern the conduct of criminal prosecutions in the United States.

The first of these great rights of the individual who is suspected of crime is his right of privacy. The powers of the police in the investigation of crime are limited —"a knock on the door at midnight" does not give the police the right to make a search solely on their own authority. Each man's privacy is protected from arbitrary intrusion by government officials.

This right to privacy gives substantial protection to our citizens against unreasonable searches of their persons, houses, papers and other belongings; against unreasonable seizures of their property and documents; and against being compelled to give evidence against themselves. These principles are specifically set forth in our federal and state constitutions. The lines separating what is reasonable in the light of the community's need for investigation of crime from what is unreasonable in the light of the individual's right to privacy, have been worked out and are embodied in our traditions and customs.

Thus, the police or other law-enforcement authorities may make legal searches and seizures if they obtain an express authorization of a judge, which is granted only on the basis of sworn evidence showing reasonable justification for each particular search and seizure. There is also authority in the police, when one has been legally arrested, to search his person and to search the place where the arrest was made in order to find and seize articles connected with the crime, or weapons and other things usable to effect an escape.

The precise lines of the compromise between the individual's right to privacy and the interest in group security vary from time to time as new inventions and devices react upon our traditions and customs. The widespread use of automobiles and telephones and the development of chemical tests to determine intoxication and paternity have led to reexamination of older traditional doctrines.

But the moral principles underlying the right to privacy are still controlling. The rule was established three hundred years ago that police and other government agents cannot force or require any person to answer their questions and thus to give evidence against himself. The discovery of truth serums and lie detectors of varying degrees of accuracy has not led to any relaxation of this rule; the police are prohibited from requiring suspects to submit to such tests. Also, wire tapping of telephone conversations is generally unlawful, and evidence procured by such wire tapping, even in the rare instances when it is permitted, may not be used on trial in the federal courts and in the courts of many states.

The police are free to question a suspect, of course, but the use of any physical or psychological coercion to force him to answer is forbidden and will render any confession thus obtained absolutely inadmissible against him. Nor can any person—whether a suspect or merely a witness—be compelled at any stage of a criminal proceeding to give evidence which would implicate him in a crime, unless he has first been given immunity from subsequent prosecution for the crime. Only thus do we believe the right to privacy can be satisfactorily protected.

Once the police have determined to institute criminal proceedings against a suspect, they must respect his right to personal freedom and personal dignity in their dealings with him. Here again a series of workable compromises has been developed over the centuries. Persons may be arrested only when they have been found committing crimes in the presence of the arresting officer, or when there is probable cause—that is, reasonable grounds—to believe them guilty of past crimes. Once arrested by the police they may be questioned, but again, physical or psychological coercion may not be used to obtain a confession or other evidence. For example, our courts have ruled that it is prohibited to use a stomach pump to retrieve narcotic drugs swallowed by the defendant before arrest. If coercive methods are used, the evidence so obtained may not be admitted against the accused in any criminal proceeding.

Prolonged imprisonment without a judicial hearing is also forbidden. A person, once arrested, must be brought before a magistrate without unnecessary delay. Here he is entitled to a prompt hearing to determine whether there is probable cause to hold him. If he is to be held, he is entitled as of right to be released on bail, unless the case is one of the few crimes which may carry the death penalty. Excessive bail may not be set. If an indigent defendant is not financially able to put up bail, other types of legal machinery are being devised to make it possible to release him safely if experience shows that the threat of a criminal prosecution for failing to surrender on demand will insure his presence at the trial.

Protection is also given to individuals against the injury to their personal reputation which would arise from an unjustified trial upon a criminal charge of which they were clearly innocent. Thus, before a man may be tried for any charge, there must be a complaint under oath charging him with a specific act prohibited by law. If the alleged crime is at all serious, he is further entitled to have the question of probable cause to justify his trial determined either by a grand jury of his fellow citizens, or (in states which have abolished the grand jury) by a judge, on the basis of sworn testimony given by witnesses who appear personally before the grand jury or judge.

Through these rules, the impact of a criminal prosecution upon an individual's dignity and reputation is cushioned with the magic touchstone of "probable cause" having to be proved at all stages.

Once probable cause to hold the accused for trial has been established, the relations between the accused and his government reach a critical point. The government is well armed with attorneys and other legal experts who know the substantive law and the rules of criminal procedure. Must the accused meet them without professional assistance?

Here is a field in which American traditions are recent and growing. The development of the right of the accused to the assistance of counsel well illustrates how these traditions change. The right of the accused to retain counsel at his own expense in a minor crime has long been recognized in England. But it was not until the early part of the nineteenth century that his right to retain counsel to represent him at all stages of investigation and trial of major crimes, called felonies, was established by statute in England. Many courts in the United States were well in advance of the English in insuring to the accused the right to retain counsel in all cases, and this right in federal cases was expressly established by the Sixth Amendment, adopted in 1791. A suspect or an accused person has the legal right to have his lawyer with him, to advise him and to speak on his behalf in court at all times.

Nevertheless, for many years this right remained an empty one for defendants who could not afford to retain counsel of their choice. Growing awareness of this fundamental unfairness led the states, and then the federal government, to make provision for assigning members of the bar to act as counsel in such cases.

It is now settled law that there is an affirmative duty

on the government to offer to assign counsel without charge to impoverished defendants in many types of cases, including all cases in which the death penalty may be exacted. This is also true in other cases where by reason of the youth of the defendant, or his mental condition, or the failure of the judge to look after his rights, a trial without counsel would not be fair. Indeed, in the federal courts and in some states, this must be done in all cases; in a number of other states it must be done in all serious cases.

The traditions of the legal profession have made this right to counsel an effective right. Counsel are entitled to adequate time to prepare the case, and personal inconvenience is not accepted as an excuse for refusal to accept an assignment. We have been fortunate in both England and the United States in having enough lawyers to carry this added responsibility, with its requirement of professional competence at the trial as well.

For the right to a fair trial is crucial. It is here that the question of guilt or innocence is finally decided. By long tradition, embodied in legally enforceable rules, the accused is entitled to a trial that is speedy and public, with just procedures, and before an impartial and disinterested tribunal. The importance of these rights, which collectively guarantee a fair trial, cannot be overstated. They deserve more than a passing comment.

In the first place, the trial must be speedy—that is, the accused may not be held in jail or even required to maintain bail for an indefinitely long period at the convenience of the government. It is a great strain to live under serious charges, and court rules giving priority to criminal cases are an essential element in the process of speedy determination of guilt or innocence.

The trial must also be public, in sharp contrast to the secret hearing of the government's case by the grand jury, which sits solely to determine probable cause. Everyone who wishes to do so is free to attend every session of a criminal trial, up to the seating capacity of the courtroom. The proceedings are publicized in the newspapers, and the court stenographer's record is open to public inspection by anyone as soon as it has been typed up.

While publicity about a trial is not a complete guarantee that it will be a fair trial, experience has taught the hard lesson that judges, jurors, prosecutors and witnesses usually behave better in public. If they do not, the publicity about their improper actions makes it possible to correct them. Indeed, the presence of newspaper reporters and members of the general public at a trial is also a protection to the government. Where a trial has been secret, it will be hard to convince the general public that a charge by the accused and his friends of unfair tactics by the judge and prosecuting officials is unfounded. This is because the only other witnesses will be the very government officials who are accused of misconduct. But such an unfounded charge by a person convicted at a public trial can never secure public acceptance, since it can be completely disproved by the unprejudiced spectators who were in attendance at the trial as representatives of the general public.

The impartiality of the tribunal itself is assured by

detailed rules governing the selection of jurors, and the grounds of disqualification of the judge. They are much the same in both civil and criminal cases. Judges and jurors are disqualified from sitting if any of their other commitments, whether through public office or private connection or emotional bias, would give them any substantial interest in the outcome of the case.

At the trial, the burden is on the government to prove the accused guilty beyond a reasonable doubt. This means that after careful consideration of the evidence, all twelve of the jurors must be so strongly convinced by the government's case that they have no reasonable doubt of the guilt of the accused. And in sustaining this burden, the prosecutor is not permitted to call the accused to give evidence, or even (in most states) to draw an adverse inference against an accused who fails to avail himself of his personal privilege to take the witness stand in his own behalf if he wishes to do so. If the accused does choose to testify, however, he is treated as any other witness. He is subject to prosecution for perjury if he lies, although such prosecutions are rare.

Finally, the primary duty of the prosecutor "is not to convict, but to see that justice is done." He may not knowingly use perjured evidence, or seek to suppress facts, or conceal witnesses capable of establishing the innocence of the accused.

Here, too, our Anglo-American traditions and customs are still in process of development. Let me give a specific instance. In a society which requires public trials, and permits free discussion of public issues, it is inevitable that violent crime will make newspaper headlines. But these same headlines may make it difficult to secure an impartial jury. In England this problem is being met by imposing reasonable restrictions on the press coverage of crime. Here in the United States, with more freedom given to the press, part of the answer is being found in a careful screening of jurors to exclude those who are apt to be influenced by publicity. It is also possible to delay the trial until public clamor has died down, or to move the trial to another part of the state where local interest is less intense. But this problem is still not wholly solved in the United States.

American law recognizes that a convicted defendant is not stripped of his human rights even after sentence. During the past hundred years, the right to decency in punishment and treatment has been developed, first through changing public opinion and tradition, and finally through court decisions. Cruel and unusual punishment is forbidden in all states. Hanging and other cruel forms of capital punishment have everywhere been displaced by more humane methods. Treatment designed to rehabilitate rather than merely to punish is more and more coming to be one of the accepted goals of the criminal law. An immense amount of effort has gone into improving the living conditions of our prisoners in jails and penitentiaries, although here progress has not been as rapid as one could wish. But there are healthy indications that as scientific methods of prediction of criminal behavior are developed, they will be used increasingly in determining sentences and eligibility for release on parole.

I have spoken of all these rights of the defendant in the terms in which they are created and defined by law. But a right which cannot be enforced may be of very little value. A final and important question must be this—do there exist effective ways of correcting errors in the criminal proceedings?

Our chief safeguard for correction of such errors is the judiciary. In all jurisdictions there exist ways of appealing any abuses to multi-judge appellate courts, which are not limited to correcting errors at law, but in most states may also set aside unreasonable decisions of issues of fact. Any person held in custody may test the legality of his detention by the historic writ of *habeas corpus*. This is an order issued by a judge requiring the officials who are holding the prisoner to permit him to appear before the court to contest the grounds for his detention. By the *habeas corpus* writ—sometimes called "the freedom writ"—persons convicted of crimes in state courts are able to obtain a review of their cases in the federal courts, and ultimately in the Supreme Court of the United States, on the ground that during the course of their trial their constitutional right of due process of law was violated.

Persons held under detention, whether before or after conviction of crime, may not be denied the right to communicate with their lawyers and friends, and to file papers in court to enforce these rights. An effective appeal to a higher court may not be made conditional upon the possession of financial resources sufficient to permit printing of the record or other financial needs test.

Before I close I want to summarize the various ways in which the agents of the state—the prosecuting attorneys and police—may be compelled by the judiciary to respect the rights of accused persons. Every judge who presides over an American trial is charged with the duty of restraining the prosecutor from unfair tactics to which he might be tempted in the heat of the trial. The judge must also exclude confessions and other evidence obtained by the police through coercion or brutality of any sort, as has already been noted.

In some cases the police may have violated the rights of the accused in other ways. He may have been illegally arrested, or held by the police after arrest for an unnecessarily long time before being brought before a judge for preliminary hearing. Evidence against him may have been illegally obtained by an unreasonable search and seizure of his property and belongings, or by unlawful wire tapping of his telephone communications.

In all these cases, the police and other officials guilty of such misconduct may be sued civilly by the accused for damages, and in many cases they are also liable to criminal prosecution. Since these deterrents have not in fact secured observance of the rights of the accused person in all cases, the further question of their specific enforcement by exclusion of any evidence obtained through governmental misconduct has necessarily been raised. During the last fifty years these considerations have led a growing number of states to rule that the trial judge must exclude all evidence thus illegally obtained. Even if this evidence had only furnished leads by which other evidence has been secured, this secondary evidence will also be excluded as "the fruit of the poisonous tree" in these states.

The Supreme Court of the United States has taken the lead in this matter. Its basic rule of practice in the federal courts, by which all illegally obtained evidence is excluded, was first enunciated in 1914. Since that time it has been extended further than in most state courts. Thus, for the past twenty years, confessions obtained by federal officials without coercion, but after the period when the accused should have been brought before a judge for preliminary hearing, have not been admissible in the federal courts. A practice is also developing by which federal judges will enjoin federal officers who have obtained evidence illegally from turning it over to the state courts.

It is still true, however, that in most state courts there is no general rule excluding evidence which has been illegally obtained. It can nevertheless be said that throughout the whole country there exists a strong and growing awareness of the need for better enforcement of the laws prohibiting oppressive police tactics, accompanied by vigorous methods which have been used for this purpose in England and in the United States.

The picture of the rights of the accused in a criminal prosecution thus shows certain broad underlying principles, upon which have been built a great mass of detailed rules, subject to change from time to time to meet changing conditions, and to accord with evolving conditions and customs. These principles, developing during a period in which Western civilization has been in a state of rapid change, have proved their worth through many periods of crisis. For our traditional and cultural heritage of due process of law has greatly inspired and influenced the lives and activities of the millions of individuals, living and dead, who have made up Anglo-American society. Rules of criminal procedure which treat human beings as individuals, and hold each one individually responsible only for his own acts, leave them free to go about their business, secure in the knowledge that they will not be unjustly punished by the state. This has had a great effect in releasing their energy for productive and imaginative ends.

Moreover, we have relied on an independent judiciary, acting in individual cases on the initiative of the parties, as the chief instrument to correct abuses in law enforcement. This has permitted us to avoid overcentralization of control in the hands of administrative agencies which might be linked politically with the police and has encouraged participation by many segments of the community in reform of the administration of criminal justice.

I should like now to close with another brief quotation which seems to me to epitomize the powerful assistance which this American ideal of individual freedom has given to the survival and growth of Western civilization. It comes from a second book which I have in my hand as I end this talk—Professor David Fellman's recent work on *The Rights of the Accused*.

"Our greatest security will be found in maintaining

our freedom. We are not free because we are strong; on the contrary, we are strong because we are free. Our whole way of life rests upon the verity of this proposition."

VI

❯❯❯·❯❯❯·❯❯❯❮❮❮·❮❮❮·❮❮❮

Paul A. Freund

THE SUPREME COURT

MORE THAN a century ago Alexis de Tocqueville remarked, with characteristic perception and clairvoy-
ance, that the major issues of American life sooner or
later appear as questions for decision by the courts. In
the succeeding years this observation has lost none of
its validity. Across the forum of the Supreme Court
there have passed, like figures in a morality play, most
of the great forces whose conflict and resolution have
been the themes of American history: the opening of
a continent and local rivalries in transportation and
trade, the expansion of commerce and business and the
pressures for its control, slavery and civil war, organized
industry and organized labor, social-welfare legislation, taxation, public ownership of public utilities, war
and compulsory military service and internal security,
church and state, a free press and public order, efficient
law enforcement and the right to a fair trial. Interests
of property and interests of personality, the most ur-
gent claims of government and the most treasured

claims of the individual, all have been arrayed before the Supreme Court for resolution. So much is true of Tocqueville's generalization.

But it would be a mistake to accept this bold outline as a faithful representation of the role of the Court. What is lacking in this picture is the feature without which the portrait becomes a caricature—the feature, that is, of a tribunal which is a court of law, with all the qualifications that this implies. For the Supreme Court exists to decide lawsuits, not to give answers to abstract questions of law, still less to render advice on political questions. The Constitution provides that the authority of the federal courts shall extend to "cases or controversies." This formula means that the jurisdiction of the federal courts can be invoked only where a person claims that a conventional legal right has been infringed. Neither the President nor Congress may seek the opinion of the Supreme Court on the validity or interpretation of a law or a proposed law outside the framework of an ordinary lawsuit; and even within such a framework a litigant may be found not to possess a conventional legal interest that would justify a judicial decision. On this ground, for example, a long and costly litigation challenging the validity of the Tennessee Valley Authority came to an end; the private power companies which brought the suit, and which possessed non-exclusive franchises, were held not to have a legal interest in questioning the authority of a competitor, whether that competitor was another private company or, as in the case itself, an agency of the federal government. Months of testimony and arguments, volumes of evidence and documents, were turned aside with four words: damage without legal injury; three words in the original Latin: *damnum absque injuria.*

In the same vein, citizens may not bring proceedings to attack a legislative measure which does not affect them in a direct and immediate way; for this reason the spending power, the power of the public purse, is largely beyond the range of judicial review. Moreover, when the Court does accept a case for decision, the decision itself will be put on the most moderate ground that is conscientiously possible. If a law can be interpreted in a way to avoid a serious question of its constitutional validity, that construction will be adopted; or if the case can be disposed of on some less heroic plane, that course will be followed. A number of recent cases in the field of internal security have been decided in this way. For example, questions of the power to deny passports to Communists, and of the necessary procedural safeguards for alleged subversives before they can be discharged from employment in national-defense industries—constitutional questions of obvious gravity and delicacy—have been avoided by decisions holding that the necessary authority for the governmental actions could not be found in the statutes of Congress.

These two aspects of the role of the Supreme Court —that it may pass judgment on some of the profoundest national issues and that it will do so only when absolutely necessary to the solution of a conventional lawsuit—mark the central paradox of the Court's function. And yet the two elements are not antithetical.

Together they help to explain the ultimate paradox of the Court's power, the power of a small group of judges, appointed for life, to set aside the acts of the representatives of the people in a democracy. The rules of "case or controversy" can be seen as the necessary corollary of this vast power—necessary for its wise exercise and its popular acceptance. By declining to give advisory opinions, the Court refrains from intrusion into the law-making process. By requiring a concrete case with litigants adversely affected, the Court helps itself to avoid premature, abstract, ill-informed judgments. By placing a decision on a non-constitutional ground whenever possible, the Court gives the legislature an opportunity for sober second thought, an opportunity to amend the statute to obviate the constitutional question, a chance to exercise that spirit of self-scrutiny and self-correction which is the essence of a successful democratic system.

So far we have said little of the positive reasons for the establishment and powers of the Supreme Court. Undoubtedly the clue lies, as does so much of American history, in the federal character of the government. The Revolution was fought because British federalism proved unadaptable to the demands of the American colonies; the American Civil War was fought because American federalism foundered on the issue of slavery. At all events, the framers of the American constitution in 1787 were familiar with the role of a final court of appeal in resolving some of the conflicts to which a federation or confederation gives rise. Appeals had been taken from the colonies to the Privy

Council in England over the authority of local government; and immediately after the Revolution, under the Articles of Confederation, it became necessary for the Congress to set up a Court of Appeal to determine disputes between the states over boundaries, the capture of vessels, and the like. The federal judiciary, authorized by article three of the Constitution, was given jurisdiction over controversies that appeared to transcend the interest of individual states: controversies between states, those to which the United States was a party, those involving ambassadors and other foreign diplomats, those between citizens of different states or between a state and a citizen of another state, and those arising under the Constitution, laws, or treaties of the United States.

At the head of the hierarchy of federal courts there was placed the Supreme Court, with appellate jurisdiction over most of these classes of cases, its original (non-appellate) jurisdiction being confined to suits in which a state or a foreign diplomat is a party. Side by side with the federal courts stand the courts of each state, whose jurisdiction somewhat overlaps that of the federal judiciary. From the beginning, Congress has given the Supreme Court appellate jurisdiction over decisions of the highest courts of the states in cases which turn on a provision of the federal constitution or of a federal law or treaty.

To put all this in less technical terms, the role of the Supreme Court in the American federal system may be taken as threefold: to maintain the supremacy of the Constitution, to assure the uniform interpretation of federal law, and to resolve legal controversies between the states themselves. It will be convenient to deal with these functions in inverse order.

First, then, controversies between states. A considerable number of these have arisen, involving in the main disputes over boundaries and the apportionment of interstate waters. In the settlement of these disputes the Court performs very much like an international tribunal, serving, as has been aptly said, as a substitute for diplomacy and war.

Next, the function of assuring the uniformity of federal law. With the great increase in social and economic legislation by Congress, much of it administered by federal bureaus and commissions, this task of the Court has assumed larger and larger importance. Laws regulating maximum hours of labor and minimum wages, guaranteeing the right of collective bargaining to labor unions, supervising the rates and practices of railroads, motor trucks, buses, and carriers by water, allocating radio and television channels, controlling the services of air carriers, prohibiting combinations in restraint of trade and unfair methods of competition—these and a host of other laws, enacted by Congress to apply to businesses that transcend state boundaries, call for interpretation that does not vary from district to district. In each state there is at least one federal court; there are eleven regional federal courts of appeals; over these federal appellate courts the Supreme Court has ultimate reviewing authority in the event of conflicting decisions among the regions.

The third function of the Court, the maintenance

of the constitutional order, is without doubt the most complex and controversial of the Court's tasks. Once again the federal system is the key to many of the problems. In the terminology of the Constitution, Congress has the power to regulate commerce among the several states, or, as it has come to be called, interstate commerce. From the time of Chief Justice Marshall continuously to the present, this grant of power has been deemed to imply a negative on the states: the states may not regulate interstate commerce. But what is comprehended in interstate commerce, and what constitutes regulation? The forms of trade are so various, the methods and objects of regulation are so manifold, that the process of adjudicating between the claims of business enterprise on the one hand and of the demands of a state on the other is a ceaseless, never-completed task for the Court.

Certain types of state legislation are easily identified as unconstitutional interferences with interstate commerce: restrictions on the importation of goods from sister states, or preferences given to the sale of local goods, are obvious discriminations condemned by the commerce clause. But the problems are not usually so simple. Suppose that a state or a municipality, claiming to act in the interest of the health of its citizens, requires that all milk sold locally shall be pasteurized in local establishments. Assume further that milk brought in from other states could in fact be pasteurized where it was shipped, but that the state of destination will not accept this as sufficient. Is such a law a legitimate measure for the protection of health, or an illegitimate interference with commerce? Suppose that a state where natural gas is produced forbids the export of that resource until the needs of its own inhabitants are met. Suppose that a state imposes a similar embargo on fresh water.

At one time the Court tried to solve these problems by classifying a particular state law either as a regulation of commerce, and therefore unconstitutional, or a regulation of health, and therefore valid. The unsatisfactory nature of this kind of analysis became manifest. The beginning of wisdom occurred when the Court recognized that such laws are regulations both of commerce and of health, and that there is no escape from the duty of weighing the relative burden on the national market against the degree of the local need, and indeed of considering whether other alternative measures, less burdensome to commerce, are available to safeguard the local interest. Applying such a criterion, the Court struck down the laws dealing with pasteurization and natural gas, and sustained the law relating to water. No purely mechanical formula could possibly explain these results.

A similar process of decision can be traced in controversies over state taxation of interstate commerce. There have been attempts to solve the problems by invoking one or another simple maxim: interstate commerce may not be taxed directly; on the other hand, interstate commerce must pay its way. The Court has been most successful in this field when it has resisted the seductive charms of such formulas, when it has recognized that the choice of one or the other conceals some very specific judgments, and has dealt with the problems on a particularistic basis. May a state impose a sales tax on an interstate sale? If so, may such a tax be imposed both by the state of market and the state of origin of the goods? Is the alternative to such double taxation the complete immunity of the sale from any state taxation? The Court has rejected these polar positions and in effect has decided that the state of market may tax, but not the state of origin. In the state of market the goods will be competing with local products which must pay a similar tax, and the burden of the tax will fall on the local consumers in that state, so that no special tribute is being exacted from outsiders. The relevance of these issues to the current development of a common market in Western Europe is surely evident. Indeed it would be surprising if there were not much of value to be found in the experience of the Supreme Court during a century and a half in striking a working balance between the needs of the individual states and the freedom of the common market.

Of course, Congress could resolve many of these problems of state authority by legislation setting metes and bounds to state authority. But the problems are so varied in their incidence, and call for such continuing scrutiny, that Congress has in the main chosen to leave them to the Court. When Congress does act, it is generally by taking over a field and subjecting it to national regulation. The acts of Congress are themselves open to challenge in the courts on constitutional grounds. From time to time the Supreme Court has frustrated acts of Congress by a restrictive view of the commerce power or by interpreting the due process clause of the Constitution as if it embodied a principle of laissez-faire, of an inviolable freedom of contract. In the last two decades, however, the Court has sustained without exception the economic measures enacted by Congress, and has cleared the way for as much congressional authority as is likely to be utilized. Even the placing of quotas on basic agricultural crops has been upheld under the power to regulate interstate commerce. In the realm of economic legislation the more important check on Congress lies in the composition of that body itself. Elected as it is by the localities, with each state represented by two members in the Senate, Congress can be expected to be sensitive to the political checks of the federal system.

Thus far, in speaking of the maintenance of the constitutional order, I have been stressing the problems of federalism—which government has authority to regulate or to tax in this or that way? The constitutional order, however, includes restraints on *all* government, through the Bill of Rights and the post-Civil War constitutional amendments; the application of these constitutes an increasingly important part of the Court's business. If I seem to give less time to these than they deserve, the reason is simply that these guarantees of fundamental rights are the subjects of other lectures in this series.

A moment ago reference was made to due process of law in the economic sphere, to the rise and fall of the notion of liberty of contract as a barrier to governmental controls. Of course the barrier was never complete.

The social interest in physical safety and health, in fair dealing, in public morals, has always been recognized as a sufficient basis for laws regulating, for example, dangerous machinery, unsanitary working conditions, and deceptive business practices. And the rates and services of business were regulated from an early day where the business was regarded by the courts as one "affected with a public interest"—enterprises such as carriers, public utilities, and banking. The newer attitude of the Supreme Court is an enlarged recognition of social interdependence and the legitimate sphere of legislative experiment. No longer must governments bring their legislation under the conventional heads of health, safety, and morals. In part the development occurred, as it often does in courts, through the use of legal fictions. When a state sought to promote the interest in aesthetics by prohibiting advertising posters on the roadside, the law was sustained, but on the ground that these advertising structures were used as a shelter to conceal vice and crime. Later, to be sure, the fiction was dropped, when it had served the purpose of fictions, as the tribute which change pays to continuity. Similarly, the class of businesses "affected with a public interest" was gradually enlarged until it came to be frankly acknowledged that there is no "closed category" of such enterprises.

Today the growing point of constitutional law is in the area of personal rights: the right to a fair hearing, rights of speech and press and assembly, and to equal protection of the laws. Even here, however, the development has not been abrupt. The school desegregation decision of 1954, for example, was preceded by a series of cases which in principle foreshadowed it: cases holding that it is a denial of equal protection of the laws for a city or state to establish by law separate white and colored residential districts, to enforce in the courts private racially restrictive property agreements, and to separate students on the basis of color in a publicly maintained university.

It is obvious that the Supreme Court has immense power in American life, that it not only reflects history but in a measure shapes history. What has been its record of popular acceptance over the years? It is hardly surprising that a tribunal possessed of this power has come into conflict with popular and political forces. A number of the strongest Presidents found themselves in disagreement with the Court. Jefferson and Jackson were critics of Chief Justice Marshall. Lincoln was unwilling to accept the Dred Scott decision as forever settling the law of slavery. Theodore Roosevelt spoke in favor of the popular recall of judges and judicial decisions. And Franklin Roosevelt, witnessing judicial vetoes of a number of his New Deal measures, sought to increase the size of the Court unless Justices retired at the age of seventy. In part such conflicts are inherent in the Court's responsibility to interpret and apply the fundamental law, to preserve the federal balance, and to hold the lawmakers to the ideals enshrined in the Constitution. In part the conflicts have been brought on by too narrow and insensitive decisions reflecting personal or parochial preconceptions, by the Court's own blunders, or what Chief Justice

Hughes once called the Court's self-inflicted wounds. And yet the resilience of the Court has been very great. It is noteworthy that of the twenty-two amendments to the Constitution only two have been directed to the overruling of Supreme Court decisions. The process of salvation has more frequently come from within the Court itself.

What, then, are the factors which have enabled the Court to discharge its responsibilities without forfeiting its prestige? They are largely to be found in the quality of the Court and especially in its methods of work. The Justices—there have been just ninety-two of them—have brought to the Court a wide range of experience and outlook. They have been drawn not only from the practicing bar and the bench but, in some of the most notable instances, from positions in public affairs. The size of the Court—six members at the beginning, and nine since 1869—has enabled all the members of the Court to participate in all its actions. Its opinions have been, characteristically, reasoned expositions and not fiats; and there has been full opportunity for individual expression of concurring and dissenting views. Decisions of the Court pay implicit tribute to the value of the dialogue in the search for what is true and just. Moreover, the Court has always held itself open for the reconsideration of doctrine, yielding, as Justice Brandeis put it, to the lessons of experience and the force of better reasoning.

The most significant aspect of the Court's work may lie in just this method and process of decision. By avoiding absolutes, by testing general maxims against concrete particulars, by deciding only in the context of specific controversies, by finding accommodations between polar principles, by holding itself open to the reconsideration of dogma, the Court at its best provides a symbol of reconciliation. Perhaps it is this blend of idealism and pragmatism that constitutes, in the end, the most notable characteristic of the judicial process as it is carried on in the American Supreme Court.

VII

~>>>~>>>~>>><<<~<<<~<<<~

Roger Fisher

THE CONSTITUTIONAL
RIGHT OF FREEDOM
OF SPEECH

WHEN WE in the United States are asked about freedom of speech we are inclined to answer "Yes, in this country we have free speech." We tend to think in terms of black and white—either/or. Either a country has freedom of speech or it does not. But that is not so. Every country has some freedom of speech: some things can be said at some times and places without prior consent and without fear of punishment. On the other hand, in no country is there complete freedom to say anything at any time in any place. The constitutional right of free speech in the United States must be understood in terms of the kinds of limitations which the government may impose, and the kinds of limitations which it may not impose. By such examples we see behind the theories and words to the values which they reflect.

The First Amendment to our Constitution provides:

> "Congress shall make no law . . . abridging the freedom of speech, or of the press; or the right of the people peacefully to assemble, and to petition the Government for a redress of grievances."

Note the language: "Congress shall make no law . . . abridging the freedom of speech. . . ." This is not a guaranty of freedom from private interference. It is a guaranty that the government may not interfere with freedom of speech. No government in this country, federal, state or local, may abridge the freedom of speech. The word "abridge" means to shorten, to limit, or to reduce in size. The freedom of speech may not be reduced by governmental action. But what is "the freedom of speech"?

First, we must look to England to see what was understood by freedom of speech at the time the United States Constitution was adopted.

Blackstone, the great English lawyer, writing in 1765, said: "The liberty of the press . . . consists in laying no previous restraint upon publications . . ."

Blackstone's notion was that freedom of speech and freedom of press protected an individual from any prior restraint upon what he said. Before speaking he need not obtain the consent of a governmental official. The government had no right to *prevent* a man from writing, publishing and distributing a pamphlet or a book.

The government could not keep ideas from being communicated. But it could, Blackstone thought, punish a man for what he had said *after* he had said it.

This did not mean that there could be no prior restraint whatever. During wartime, for example, the government might, in order to keep military secrets, censor what a reporter sent to his newspaper. The circumstances in which the government might properly impose a prior restraint were, however, closely limited. The same is true today. In general, a man must be allowed to say whatever he pleases even though, in some circumstances, he may later be punished for having said it.

The difference in effect between prior restraint and subsequent punishment is greater than might at first appear. If a government official has the administrative power to prevent a book from seeing the light of day, on the grounds, for example, that it is indecent, he will tend to err on the side of suppression. For if he should allow a doubtful book to be published, some would be sure to criticize him; but if he should suppress the book, only the author would be disappointed; the public would never know what it had not seen. Also, the censor would tend to suppress books which criticized him, or which criticized the government. The healthy light of criticism would thus be kept from areas where it was needed. However, if the only means of curtailing free speech is by punishment after the speech has been given or after the book has been printed, there is less opportunity for governmental abuse. The speech for which the man is being punished will be publicly known. The book will have been distributed, and all can tell whether the government is abusing its power. All can tell whether the government is unjustly punishing a man simply for criticizing the government, or whether it is properly enforcing the law.

To some it may appear that to rely on punishment is to lock the barn door after the horse has gone. But the fear of punishment does deter most illegal conduct. It is a premise of our idea of freedom of speech that we must not allow the government to impose a prior restraint on what is spoken or published, for otherwise governmental power may be abused and the people may not know that this power is being abused.

But freedom of speech within the United States today means far more than it did to Blackstone. The First Amendment to the Constitution not only makes it unlawful for the government to prevent someone from speaking or publishing, it also limits the circumstances under which the Government may punish a man for what he has already said or written. The founding fathers of this country wanted there to be unrestricted discussion of public affairs. The First Amendment was intended to make prosecutions for criticism of the government, where there was no incitement to law-breaking, forever impossible.

Fundamental among the purposes of the First Amendment is the role of free expression in the democratic process. Free expression is a means of developing public opinion. Free expression is an aid to an intelligent choice. And free expression provides an opportunity to make a choice. New and better ideas are most likely to be developed in a community which allows free discussion of any ideas. Without discussion who can be sure which ideas are right and which ideas are wrong? Finally, freedom of expression serves as an outlet for resentments and hostilities that otherwise might find more dangerous expression.

Speech, of any kind, must be free and must go unpunished—unless there is some good reason for punishment. Our law of free speech is thus largely a delineation between the kinds of reasons which are good enough to justify controls on freedom of speech, and those that are not. Some interests have been found to justify restrictions on freedom of expression; others have not. Free speech in the United States depends not only upon theory, but upon facts. And it is best understood in terms of the facts.

Illustrations of the boundaries of free speech may be divided roughly into three categories: first, circumstances in which the government may require one to say only the truth, or to disclose the whole truth; second, cases in which one's speech, while not an incitement to crime, may be limited to avoid disturbing the community in one way or another; and, finally, those cases in which speech is an incitement to criminal conduct.

First, there are circumstances in which a speaker may not be free to lie. He must tell the truth. In this category are the laws which impose civil liability for slander and libel. You may not call a man a thief unless he is a thief. You may not say that food bought from a certain store will make one sick unless it is true. Freedom of speech does not include the right to damage a man's reputation or his business by false statements.

But, in order to allow full discussion of political affairs, there is an important exception here. In many states, you may freely make any statement regarding a public official, a candidate for office, or other men in public life so long as you *believe* it to be true. Even if it turned out later to be false, you would not be liable for damage that your statement may have caused. Here, allowing good faith, criticism of public officials is considered more important than insisting upon exact truth.

In commercial transactions, a buyer or a seller is not free to say whatever he wishes. He may be required to speak truthfully. While free speech includes the right to say that glass is more valuable than diamonds, it does not include the right to say that a piece of glass is a diamond and to deceive someone into paying a high price for it.

In various cases you must not only tell the truth but must tell all the truth. A corporation may not sell its stock on the basis of half-truths. It is subject to detailed regulation requiring it to disclose its assets, who its officers are, and so forth. Even in the purely political field the government has imposed some restrictions of this full-disclosure sort, limiting the anonymous political advertisement. And a person who is *hired* to make statements on behalf of a foreign government must register and disclose that he is making the statements as a foreign agent and must disclose the amount that he has been paid as agent.

These examples, then, illustrate the first category of restrictions affecting freedom of expression—those which limit the telling of falsehood or the telling of half-truths.

Into a second category of restraints upon speech which are permitted under the Constitution may be placed all those restraints which are designed to prevent us from disturbing the community or disturbing our neighbors.

Obviously, the fact that a neighbor or the community would be disturbed is not always ground enough in itself to justify prohibiting things from being said. But possible disturbance to the community does justify limitations on where or when or how things are said. In each case the legislature, administrative officers and, finally, the Supreme Court, must weigh the seriousness of the restraint on freedom of expression against the community interest being served. Again, the best way to explain where the line is drawn is to illustrate with cases where speech, short of that which incites to criminal conduct, may be restricted.

Justice Oliver Wendell Holmes once said: "The most stringent protection of free speech would not protect a man in falsely shouting fire in a theater and causing a panic." In other instances the immediate disturbance to the community is not so great, and nonetheless a government may impose some restraints. A community may prevent signs from being erected along a scenic roadway, even though this limits the means by which political or other kinds of messages may be communicated to the public. A town may impose regulation upon the use of trucks which are equipped with loud speakers—it may, for example, limit the loud playing of music on such a sound truck. But it could not prohibit their use entirely. If ideas are to be freely communicated we must put up with some disturbance. Tranquillity is not the most important consideration.

The Supreme Court has held that a town, without violating the First Amendment, could prohibit door to door solicitation even though to do so precluded one means of distributing magazines. On the other hand, the Supreme Court has also held that a community's interest in keeping its streets clean is not sufficiently great to justify a prohibition on passing out leaflets.

An Illinois statute designed to lessen racial tension makes it a crime to distribute any publication which "exposes the citizens of any race, color, creed or religion to contempt or derision." In 1952 this law was considered by the Supreme Court and held to be valid. Obviously the law did impose some restrictions on freedom of expression, but the Court found that the State of Illinois might properly provide laws which protected the reputation of a group, just as the normal laws of slander and libel protect the reputation of an individual.

Currently we are engaged in a controversy over the extent to which the government may limit freedom of the press in order to prevent the circulation of obscene literature. It is established that books or magazines which deliberately deal with sex in a disgusting or revolting way may be prohibited if they are bad enough. Here, public morality and protecting people from being assaulted by offensive material are considered more important than the freedom to sell dirty books. But we are having difficulty solving the problem of who should draw the line, and how. There are always some publishers, with various motives, who produce material in the border-line area. A genuine nudist magazine urging a healthy life in the open sunshine is clearly permissible even though it contains photographs of people with no clothes on. But may a community suppress a magazine which looks similar, but which contains little more than pictures of naked people and which is sold only because of its erotic interest?

Another instance in which speech may be punished is where the speech injures the ability of the judicial system to operate. The administration of law depends upon the ability of a court system to operate impartially. The publisher of a newspaper which seeks to influence the judge or jury in a particular case may be punished for contempt of court. This does not mean that a judge is free from criticism. Newspapers in the United States have great freedom to comment on a pending trial. A majority of the Supreme Court has supported the view that a newspaper is free to attack a court so long as that attack does not constitute an "imminent . . . threat to the administration of justice." A court's decision may be called "outrageous." And a newspaper which made an unfair report of a pending case and charged a judge with being "high handed" and committing a "travesty on justice" was unanimously held by the Supreme Court to be immune from punishment for having said so.

The major issue in the law of free speech in the United States has been, How much freedom is there to criticize the government? This question leads us to our third category of kinds of speech which may be limited, that is speech which incites others to commit crimes. That, basically, is the standard which the government must meet if it seeks to limit political speech.

I do not have time to review the history behind the development of what we call the clear-and-present-danger test. There were times in this country, particularly right after our revolution and again during the first World War, when men were punished for saying things critical of the government, because the words were said with the purpose of interfering with the government or because the words were found to have a tendency to interfere with the government. But it is now established that that is not enough; the government must prove more before it can punish a man for what he has said. In 1919 Justice Holmes, speaking for a unanimous Supreme Court, first articulated the clear-and-present-danger test. He said:

> "The question in every case is whether the words used are used in such circumstances and are of such nature as to create a clear and present danger that they will bring about the substantive evils that Congress has a right to prevent."

The problem of drawing this line—the edge of free speech—is illustrated by two recent cases involving group activities by Communist Party members. In the first of these cases, in 1951, a group of top members of the Communist Party within the United States were found guilty by a jury of violating a statute. The statute made it a crime to conspire to encourage the overthrow by force and violence of the Government of the United States, with the intent to cause its overthrow. The Communist leaders contended that they had been simply exercising their right of free speech, and that their speaking and writing activities had not created a clear and present danger of overthrowing the government.

The Supreme Court upheld the conviction, although the judges could not agree on any one opinion. Basically, a majority of the Court believed that there was ample evidence that the defendants had caused a substantial threat to national order and security. Although the likelihood of an actual overthrow of the government was remote, even an attempted overthrow by force and violence would be sufficiently serious so that speech which incited people to such an attempt could be punished.

But this decision of the Supreme Court does not mean that Communists can be locked up in jail for expressing their views. In the second case, involving the trial of leaders of the Communist Party of California, the jury had found that the defendants had urged force and violence as a means of overthrowing and destroying the Government of the United States. The jury had also found that the defendants had taught not merely the desirability of overthrowing the government but the necessity and duty of doing so.

Nevertheless, the Supreme Court held that the defendants could *not* be punished for such teaching and urging. Although the Court was interpreting the statute, the decision does, I believe, reflect the requirements of the Constitution. The Court found that even advocating the overthrow of the government by force and violence was not a crime so long as the speaker was simply favoring the abstract doctrine or theory. Speakers could not be punished for what they said unless they had been inciting others to unlawful conduct, and unless the circumstances were such as to reasonably justify fear that action would occur.

Even if a speaker intends to accomplish the overthrow of the government and even if his speaking has a tendency to generate action, the speech is permissible so long as it is in fact advocating doctrine rather than inciting to action. Thus, the government may interfere least with speech that is critical of the government. We give our government great power. To prevent it from abusing that power and to lessen the chance of its making mistakes, the government is not allowed to limit criticism of the government or to punish those who criticize it. One may throw words at the government without limit. One may say that another revolution is justified. The government may step in only when the speaker is inciting others to violence and there is a significant chance—a "clear and present danger"—that violence will result.

Theoretical talk about freedom of speech may give the impression of a static state of affairs. As I said at the beginning, freedom is not an "either/or" proposition. In the United States there is a continuing process of adjustment taking place. Federal, state and local governments are constantly adopting new rules. In the name of serving the interests of the community as a whole, these rules impose various restraints upon the freedom of the individual. Many of us, for our own sakes and because we believe it best for the country, often attack these restrictions. Sometimes the restrictions are said to be unwise. Sometimes they are said to be unconstitutional. Both through the legislatures and through the courts the constant process of adjusting these competing interests takes place. What is most significant is that this adjustment between liberty and restriction takes place in the open where there is full freedom to criticize the government. The one freedom that is most important is the freedom to criticize our elected representatives for the restrictions they impose upon freedom. We must have the freedom to argue for more freedom.

Let me illustrate that point by exercising some free speech here and now. The Government of the United States today imposes serious restrictions on the liberty of Americans to go to the mainland of China. Elected and appointed officials, acting in what they believe to be the interests of the country as a whole, prevent American citizens from traveling to Peking or Shanghai, or elsewhere in Communist China. This restriction limits my ability to talk directly with people in China to whom I might wish to talk. It limits the ability of newspaper reporters to gather information about China. Such information should be known and discussed if the United States is going to reach wise decisions about our future policy toward China. The governmental restriction limits the ability of people in this country to meet and associate with persons in a vast and important part of the world. I believe the restriction now being imposed by the United States Government is contrary to the principles of the First Amendment. I would argue in a court that the restriction is unconstitutional. I am firmly convinced that it is unwise and a serious mistake.

But the truly significant thing about free speech in this country is not the restriction on travel to China. The important thing is that I am free to speak against that restriction. Anywhere in the United States I may criticize our officials and their policies. I may urge different policies—without prior restraint and without fear of punishment. I may urge the desirability of a different form of government. The traditions of free speech are so strong that even on a radio program financed by the government, I am free to criticize the government. And I am confident that the government will broadcast this criticism, because the policy of the government is that of the First Amendment to our Constitution: namely, that the country is most likely to pursue a wise policy if there is free discussion of public affairs.

VIII

➤➤➤-➤➤➤-➤➤➤❮❮❮-❮❮❮-❮❮❮

Arthur E. Sutherland

CONSTITUTIONAL

RIGHTS OF

RACIAL MINORITIES

IN THE UNITED STATES

LINGERING CONSEQUENCES of human slavery—consequences not entirely eliminated even today, despite ninety-five years that have passed since our Constitution forbade all such servitude—have presented in our time to the United States its most troublesome racial problems. We have had other ethnic frictions, of course. Voluntary migration of over forty million people from every part of the globe to our country has made some such difficulties inevitable. But our main racial problem began in 1619 when a Dutch ship brought to our shores a cargo of Africans. The captives were sold as slaves at Jamestown, Virginia. This original wrong, and the succeeding wrongs which stemmed from the same human indignity, have brought trouble and sorrow throughout the following centuries for the people of the thirteen English colonies on the American seaboard, and for the United States into which these colonies organized themselves in 1776.

An appraisal of the present constitutional position of racial minorities in the United States must be made with some recollection of these three and a half centuries of history. Our constitutional ideals have not been stationary. They have, we hope, improved with the development of our moral concepts. But for some members of any society time works slowly. Some traces of old social attitudes still survive, some consequential residues of the beliefs of past centuries still remain among us, here and there, almost a century after a bitter war ended our human slavery. Our constitutionalism is partly a system of morals. And moral growth is a slow process.

Social and legal attitudes in the United States vary in space, as well as in time. A feature of our Constitution which must be remembered in appraising today's problems of racial minorities is the federal structure of our republic. Federalism is part of our deep commitment to a theory of limited government. Among us a cherished political doctrine insists that governmental power be restrained rather than absolute. And one means to this end is a measure of local autonomy, constitutionally guaranteed. Respecting some matters of government, our nation is divided in fifty separate polities, fifty states, each semi-independent as to those laws thought to govern matters essentially local rather than national. Schools, hotels, theaters have customarily been considered such local, state-controlled matters. Each state has its own elected governor, its own legislature and its own system of courts. In the same city often are found governmental officers of the central government and officers of the states, each performing his own separate duties in neighboring buildings. Of course, the Constitution of the United States and federal statutes passed under its authority are supreme. But in matters which the Constitution leaves to state control, state governments have the last word. This toleration of local autonomy, within reasonable limits, is one expression of our distrust of an all-powerful central rule.

Here then, I undertake a brief survey of these two great facts in our constitutional story: change for the better, during many generations, of our moral, and so of our legal, attitudes toward our fellow-men of different races; and the effect of this change on the peculiar, mosaic-like governmental structure of component states which makes up our federal union.

As the eighteenth century closed, people in many of the thirteen American states came to feel that the capture and sale of Africans, often by African tribesmen, and their importation for slavery was a great moral wrong. Our southern states, however, were largely dependent on slave labor for the conduct of their plantations. Deep sectional differences thus developed; resulting constitutional compromises are apparent in the now obsolete slavery provisions of the 1789 Constitution. One such clause permitted importation of slaves until 1808. But this provision did not prevent the Congress from enacting regulations governing the conduct of United States shipping. And so from 1794 on, the Congress imposed heavier and heavier penalties on any citizen engaging in the overseas slave trade. From January 1, 1808, the Congress prohibited all importation of slaves. In 1820 our Congress by statute treated overseas slave trading as piracy, punishable by death.

The legislatures of some of our states, too, began to pass antislave-trade laws. For example, the State of Maryland by a statute of 1796, provided that any Negro brought into that state for sale or residence should become free. State courts enforced such laws, and their judgments freeing slaves were affirmed by the Supreme Court of the United States.

Unfortunately, the law is a complicated business. In 1857 a man named Dred Scott, held as a slave, brought suit claiming that he had become a free man when his owner had removed him into the northerly frontier territory, once part of French Louisiana, in which, by an Act of the United States Congress, slavery had been forever prohibited. The Supreme Court of the United States, to which Scott's case finally came, held that because of his slave ancestry, he was not a "citizen," and so was under certain procedural disabilities. It further held that the Act of Congress purporting to abolish slavery in the northerly territory was beyond the constitutional powers of the central government. The unfortunate Scott was thus neither a citizen nor a free human being.

Dred Scott's case, a symbol of the evils of slavery, became a rallying cry for antislavery sentiment in the northern part of the United States. Memory of Scott's case was one of the influences in the 1860 election of the antislavery President Abraham Lincoln. Civil war between the northern and southern states broke out early in 1861.

Four years of bitter conflict, costly in lives on both sides, ended with the defeat of the South; and three amendments to the federal Constitution soon wrote the result into our fundamental law. The Thirteenth Amendment of 1865 provided that slavery should not exist within the United States or in any place subject to its jurisdiction. The Fourteenth Amendment of 1868 provided that all persons born or naturalized in the United States should be citizens of the United States and of the state where they reside, and that no state should abridge the privileges or immunities of any citizen of the United States nor deprive any person of life, liberty, or property without due process of law, nor deny to any person equal protection of the laws. In 1870 the Fifteenth Amendment provided that rights of the citizens of the United States to vote should not be denied or abridged by any state or by the United States by reason of race, color, or previous condition of servitude.

The constitutional history of racial minorities since 1870 has been written in the judicial construction of these amendments. Within fifteen years after the end of the Civil War, Americans of African descent began to establish in the courts their right to equality in the

administration of justice and equality in voting procedures. Our courts declared unconstitutional and invalid any state laws to the contrary. Most such cases,
naturally, originated in states where slavery had pre-
vailed and where the non-white population was substantial. In 1880, for example, the Supreme Court upheld a criminal charge against a Virginia state judge for
failing to select Negroes as jurors. Administration of
justice was to be color-blind.

The Fourteenth Amendment is subject to one important qualification. While that amendment forbids
the states to discriminate unjustly against racial groups,
its terms contain no prohibition against discrimination by private citizens. The federal Congress, under
our theory of limited powers, can only legislate concerning those matters constitutionally entrusted to it,
and the Fourteenth Amendment grants to Congress
no authority to make laws against private racial discrimination; it forbids public, not private, injustice.
An 1883 case, giving effect to this principle, was a dis-
appointment for the former slaves and their children.
The Supreme Court had before it an Act of Congress
forbidding racial discrimination by hotels, theaters and
passenger carriers, none of them operated by the public authorities. The Court held the Act of Congress invalid because it exceeded the federal powers; it attempted to regulate wrongs not perpetrated by a state.

In 1886 the Supreme Court, this time applying the
"equal protection clause" of the Fourteeneth Amendment in favor of some Chinese nationals, held that a

California administrative official was constitutionally required to observe racial impartiality in granting or withholding licenses to conduct laundries. Chinese, alike with others, were entitled to earn a living.

In 1896 the Supreme Court faced a particularly difficult problem. A non-white railway passenger, traveling within Louisiana, challenged the consitutional validity of a statute of that state requiring railroads to provide "equal but separate" accommodations for the different races. The Supreme Court upheld the state law on the premise that separation of races was not inconsistent with their equal treatment.

That decision was not overruled until 1954; but during the interval the constitutional position of the minority races improved in other important respects. They made notable progress in political standing. From 1885 on, the Court sturdily upheld the voting rights of non-whites. For example, in the United States, selection of candidates who stand for election to public office is ordinarily made in "primary elections," in which members of the political parties vote for those whom they wish as their party candidates in the final election. In some states, the predominant party undertook to limit party membership to white citizens, thus excluding non-whites from participation in primary elections, and effectively preventing them from influencing the final election. In a series of judgments during the thirty years following 1925 the Supreme Court struck down all such "white primary" devices.

In 1946 the Supreme Court found in the "commerce

clause" of the Constitution a weapon to use against some "equal but separate" state laws. The Constitution entrusts to the central government control of commerce "among the several states." The Supreme Court held state "equal but separate" railway or omnibus laws invalid when applied to passengers on a journey in more than one state. Such a state travel-segregation law, if enforced at the state border, would oblige travelers to rearrange their seating and would thus interfere with interstate commerce, which is the peculiar concern of the federal government. So in 1946, on interstate journeys, "equal but separate" ceased to be the rule.

The Supreme Court made other great advances toward racial equality by a series of decisions holding unconstitutional any attempt by law to restrict non-whites to segregated residential areas. In 1917 that Court held invalid a city ordinance which, in effect, established by law some city blocks solely for the residence of whites, and others solely for non-whites. Some private persons, who were buying and selling houses, tried to avoid the effect of this judgment by writing in their deeds of conveyance a requirement that the premises never be occupied by any but white residents. In 1948 the Supreme Court frustrated this device; it held unconstitutional the judicial enforcement of any such private bargain. All branches of government, the judicial as well as the legislative and executive, are forbidden to have a hand in restricting the choice of residence of any of our people.

Meantime a series of courtroom contests went on over the provisions of law, in seventeen states and in the District of Columbia, permitting or requiring the maintenance of "equal but separate" facilities for public education. In a number of cases involving state universities the Supreme Court applied the requirement of equality with much strictness, directing that such public institutions, as a condition of racial separation, be in fact equal. The steady success of non-white citizens in so many different types of constitutional lawsuits began to suggest that before long the 1896 doctrine of "equal but separate" would itself be repudiated. The Supreme Court of the United States is not bound to follow its previous decisions when it becomes convinced that they were mistaken, and so there was a constitutional possibility of ending the legality of all "equal but separate" statutes.

Exactly this occurred on May 18, 1954, a notable date in our constitutional history. The Supreme Court on that day decided cases concerning "equal but separate" public schools in four states and in the federal District of Columbia. In all these cases that Court gave judgment in favor of school children who were protesting against compulsory attendance at segregated schools. It overruled its own 1896 precedent which had established the doctrine of "equal but separate." Shortly thereafter the Court rejected "equal but separate" laws governing local omnibuses and such places of public recreation as municipal golf courses and bathing beaches. The Supreme Court thus by 1956 established the constitutional invalidity of any law, state or national, requiring that non-white people keep to themselves.

The difficult constitutional progress of racial minorities in the United States since the historic decisions of 1954 can only be understood by keeping in mind the substantial degree of local governmental independence provided by our federal system. The ancient attitude toward non-whites still persists among many white citizens in some of the seventeen states where State law had long segregated the schools. In the State public educational systems schools are not maintained by federal, but by state officials. Such schools are regulated by laws passed by State legislatures. The State legislators are elected by constituents who, in a certain number of States, resent the Supreme Court's 1954 judgments, and are eager to find ways to avoid or delay compliance. Thus despite the Supreme Court's unequivocal declarations, practical problems of enforcement remain.

In justice to our people I should point out that a substantial degree of compliance with the desegregation decrees has in fact occurred. As soon as the Supreme Court ruled against segregated schools, the President of the United States directed that the District of Columbia desegregate at once. That area, of course, is entirely controlled by the national government; the District, containing the capital of the Union, falls within no state jurisdiction. In a majority of the seventeen segregated states, gradual desegregation began at once. In eight of the seventeen, there was delay. Three of these originally recalcitrant eight states, urged by subsequent Court decrees, have now begun the process of desegregation in part of their schools. In another of the eight—Louisiana—there is now substantial enrollment of non-whites in those state colleges formerly maintained for white students only. But in five of our fifty states the opportunities for delay, which are inherent in state autonomy, up to this time (1960) still obstruct implementation, in the lower schools, of the Supreme Court's 1954 opinion.

To those who are unfamiliar with the operation of our federal union, and with the theory of limited government under which we rule ourselves, it may seem inexplicable that our great and powerful nation, which has spoken through its Constitution and its Supreme Court against racial discrimination by any state, still delays forcible requirement of obedience by several of its states. But law in action differs from law in theory. A judicial decree, strictly speaking, operates only on the persons summoned to court. And thus far, comparatively few of the many thousands of state and local school officials in these areas where desegregation is unpopular have been summoned. Additional proceedings are continually being started, but all this takes much time. Practical human difficulties retard the transformation of custom among millions of people. The remarkable fact is that so many have complied, not that a comparatively small number still resist. Two years ago, when in Little Rock, Arkansas, the local and state authorities appeared to be using force to oppose the national will in desegregation, the

President at once sent United States troops who promptly restored order without shooting. Little Rock was, fortunately, an isolated instance. Traditionally we proceed by persuasion, not by force.

The distant observer may ask why the federal Congress does not pass more laws to enforce the Constitution as construed by the Supreme Court. Such legislation has, indeed, been considered in the Congress during recent sessions. When such a statute is enacted, federal agents can be sent to the recalcitrant states to take appropriate measures. In 1957 the Congress passed just such a law to prevent local obstruction of voting. But as yet the national legislature has not provided federal enforcement of state school desegregation. Perhaps our Congress has waited in hope that the few resisting states will soon see the light.

This hope is not misplaced. The southern United States is changing rapidly. Its economy is turning from traditional concentration on agriculture to much manufacture and commerce. This change opens up new economic opportunities for technical employment of many non-white citizens who in the past have been field hands or unskilled laborers. Churches have used their influence for racial justice. Most important of all, political participation by non-whites is increasing. We move ahead.

In 1776, our Declaration of Independence expressed an ideal of human equality then unachieved. It recited:

"We hold these truths to be self-evident, that all men are created equal, that they are endowed by their Creator with certain unalienable Rights, that among these are Life, Liberty and the pursuit of Happiness. That to secure these rights, Governments are instituted among Men, deriving their just powers from the consent of the governed . . ."

We only now seem to approach realization of that ideal among races. We can well hope that the next generation will find our whole nation believing, with that Declaration, as a truth ". . . self evident; that all men are created equal. . . ."

IX

Louis L. Jaffe

ADMINISTRATIVE LAW

ADMINISTRATIVE LAW governs and controls the conduct of executive officers—the President, governors of states, cabinet members, department heads, and lesser federal, state and local officials; including boards such as the Interstate Commerce Commission, the state public utility commissions, licensing authorities and the many other so-called administrative agencies which regulate our economic and political life.

Administrators and administrative agencies are often associated in the public mind with arbitrariness, corruption and bureaucracy. But they must be judged in perspective. Government, whether by legislator, executive, or judge, can only be accomplished through individuals. Each individual will have his own conceptions of public good and his own personal purposes. And so he will be caught (sometimes quite unconsciously) in a conflict between proper and improper motives, between motives which the law allows and those which it does not. This is more likely to be true in the case of an administrator than a judge, because an administrator is usually given by law a greater scope for action and is under pressure from interested groups "to get things done." Now one of the prime objectives of administrative law is to establish guiding principles and procedures to control the wayward impulses of officials—"to keep them in line"—and yet not discourage their initiative.

Administrative law is often thought of as something new and alien to our system. There is a certain truth in this, as we shall see, but it is exaggerated. For hundreds of years we have had officials of all sorts whose actions directly control our purses and our persons, who have decided how much taxes we must pay, whether we could go into the liquor business, become lawyers, etc. And during all this time the law courts have heard complaints that these officials were acting contrary to law. The courts established principles which dealt with such questions as who could complain and when and on what grounds. For example: an innkeeper is charged with serving liquor to minors in violation of law. The licensing authorities take no steps to revoke his license. May any citizen go into a court for an order compelling the licensing authorities to proceed against the offender? Or must the complaining individual have a special interest? If he must have a special interest, what kind of interest must it be? A parent of minor children? A competing innkeeper? These questions raise the more general question whether administrative law exists primarily to enable the citizen to control public officials or primarily to enable individuals who have been injured by wrongful action to secure redress. It would take a whole book to answer this in detail; it is fair to say that the emphasis has been on protecting injured individuals, but that the courts often, though not always, will entertain actions by citizens and citizen groups.

Our innkeeper example can be used to show other kinds of questions with which our subject deals. If the licensing board decides to revoke a license, can it act on information collected by interviewing people or must it hold a hearing at which the evidence is formally presented through witnesses and at which the innkeeper is given an opportunity to cross-examine them and present contradictory testimony? Suppose there is in question, not the revocation of a license but an application for a new license. Must the applicant be given a hearing before being turned down? The law does not give a single answer to these questions concerning the right to a hearing. In revocations there is usually, but not for all kinds of licenses, such a right; in applications there sometimes is and sometimes is not. The law here seeks to strike a fair balance between the interests of the individual and the interests of the public in effective administration.

Now rules of this sort are what we generally mean by administrative law. They were brought over from England and have fortunately been with us ever since. But in the latter part of the last century, administrative law entered into a new and controversial phase. In the medieval and early modern period of Western Europe the state regulated the economy—its prices, wages, production—in considerable detail. In 1776, Adam Smith in his famous book *The Wealth of Nations* argued the thesis that this regulation strangled initiative and limited rather than increased production and wealth. People should, he argued, be left to carry on business as they chose. This "laissez-faire" philosophy, as it was called, swept Europe and America, and state regulation was substantially reduced though never completely abandoned.

Toward the end of the nineteenth century farmers, workers, small businessmen and certain professionals and intellectuals, distressed by depressions and poverty, traced their trouble to the unrestrained economic power of the banks, railroads and large corporations. They demanded that these monopolies be broken up or that their prices and services be regulated. Thus began our modern era of a privately owned capitalist economy subjected to government regulation at carefully chosen points. Monopolies were to be broken up in order to restore competition, or where that was not possible, then charges and services were to be controlled in order to assure a fair price and equal treatment to customers. By state and federal statutes enacted over a period from 1870 to the present, there came under regulation railroads, ships and buses; gas, electricity and telephone; banks, stockbrokers and investment houses; grain elevators, stockyards and exchanges. Much of this came about before 1933: state utility legislation beginning in 1870, and federal regulation of the railroads in 1887, of monopolies in 1890, of the banks in 1914. The depression of 1933 and the

New Deal added important new areas: control of securities, stock exchanges, labor relations, farm prices and production, trucking and natural gas.

It will be noted that much of this regulation is by the separate states rather than by the federal government. The localities, too, as with zoning and building restrictions, for example, are engaged in administrative regulation. We are no longer a laissez-faire society. Administrative agencies and officials operate a vast and a pervasive body of regulation in the form of general rules and day-to-day decisions which in scope and number probably exceed the work of legislatures and courts.

But what has all this to do with administrative law? The answer is that most of this regulation has been put into effect by administrative agencies, some of which were specially established to do one or more of these jobs. Thus the administrative agencies came to share both the kudos and the opprobrium attached to social reform. These agencies have usually been given very broad, loosely defined powers. The utility agencies, for example, have been given power to set "reasonable" rates (prices) for gas, electricity, transportation and certain other industries which, though in private hands, are of public concern, but without any precise statutory definition of what is "reasonable." Lawyers attacking these statutes argued that for all practical purposes the agencies were being given power to make laws; this they said was contrary to the state and federal constitutions which gave the power to make laws to the legislatures. In some cases the courts have upheld the argument that the power delegated to the agency was too broad, but on the whole they have allowed the agencies to be given very broad powers.

As a consequence, administrative agencies have important policy-making powers over the conduct of the industries or activities which they regulate. They are also given power in certain fields to make binding decisions that there has been a violation of the law. The National Labor Relations Board, for example, has power to investigate a charge that an employer has discharged an employee because of the employee's union activity, and if after a hearing it finds that the charge is proven, to order the employer to re-employ him and pay lost wages. Some lawyers have claimed that under our tradition, courts, not officials, should make such decisions. It is true that historically more often than not such decisions have been the province of courts. Yet our example of license revocations attests to the fact that administrative officers have for centuries made decisions which may be called "judicial" in character.

But why should these tasks not be done by legislatures and courts rather than by administrative agencies? There are a number of answers. For many such tasks the legislature does not have either the time or the proper organization. It can, for example, make the big decision to subject railroad rates to regulation, but not the day-to-day decisions required in determining whether each of the ten thousand rates is "reasonable." On the other hand, the courts are not equipped to do this either. We need an organization which makes the job its specialty, which becomes "expert" and which keeps the whole undertaking under continuing consideration. An administrative agency is different from a court; it not only hears and decides complaints, such as, for example, that this or that rate is unreasonable, but it is authorized and has the responsibility to proceed without complaint whenever it believes something is wrong, to make charges against an individual on its own initiative and then to decide whether those charges are true. It collects statistics, undertakes studies, makes recommendations to Congress for new legislation—tasks that courts are not set up to do and should not do. In short, an agency "administers" the law. Not all agencies have every one of these powers. They vary greatly, but most of them have some "administrative" responsibilities which are thought to be useful in carrying out the tasks assigned to them.

Much of the protest against administrative agencies which is made on the ground of violation of our legal and political traditions is motivated by hostility to the underlying policy of the legislation itself. But that does not mean that the protest is unsound: it is understandable that one does not complain about unfair procedure unless he is hurt. It is part of our tradition that where decisions seriously affect interests of individuality, whether interests of property or personality, the affected person should be given a fair hearing. This means that so far as possible the law should be correctly determined and the facts correctly found. The party must be informed of the claim made against him so that he may test whether the claim against him is well-founded in law; he must know the evidence on which the charge is based so that he is in a position to point out its weaknesses and present evidence to the contrary. Furthermore, the official decision-maker should have a "judicial" frame of mind: he should strive to make a decision on the evidence presented rather than on his own private view of the case, his own preconceptions or prejudices.

These conditions of fairness are not by and large so completely realized by administrative agencies as they are by courts. The agencies, as we have said, are responsible for developing policy. They and their professional staffs have become committed to certain points of view. When the agency comes to decide a particular case, these policy positions ("biases" some critics would call them) may influence its view of the law and the facts. This may be even more true where the agency itself initiates and "prosecutes" a proceeding. The danger of prejudgment is somewhat increased by the fact that the deciding officers customarily consult their staff before deciding and sometimes delegate to them the making of the decision. The risk of prejudgment is thus increased because the permanent staff may have more fixed policy views than the commissioners, and the consultation in the absence of the affected party may give the staff an advantage.

A great battle has raged over this issue. The proponents of the agencies believe that this kind of expert "institutional" decision, which is the product of a staff rather than one or more named deciders, is a necessary condition of effective administration and that its dangers are exaggerated. Legislature and courts have placed some restriction on this practice. Where the proceeding is predominantly "accusatory" they have sometimes required that the agency divide its staff into prosecutors and deciders and have forbidden exchanges of views between the two staffs. Such a requirement would be applicable, for example, where an agency charges that a licensee has violated the law and that his license should therefore be revoked. In addition to such procedural prohibitions, we must not forget, as we have pointed out, that the courts can keep the agencies within the bounds of legality. A court will set aside agency action where the agency's policy is not warranted by law or it is not supported by sufficient evidence. But judicial control over administrative action is limited. The courts will not for the most part substitute their own judgment where (as is so often the case) a policy or fact decision could reasonably be made either way. This means that even though the court, had it the power to make the original decision, would have decided the case the other way, it will not set aside the agency decision.

The usual criticism of the agencies is that they seek more and more power, or that they exercise power in a biased and highhanded fashion. But today a different complaint is being heard in some quarters. It is said that the regulators have been taken into camp by the people they regulate. There is probably truth in this and probably it is to some degree inevitable. In the first enthusiastic flush of reform the agency is fired with zeal, and the embattled industry will fight every inch of the way. But regulation is a long-time, day-by-day undertaking. Over the years the opposing staffs see a great deal of each other; they "sit around the table," and they come to "understand" each other. Together they build a world and come to have a stake in it. Much good is thus accomplished, reasonable concessions made, unnecessary, costly, time-consuming battles are foregone. But the agency may become a captive of its own hard-won solutions, insensitive to new claims, more sympathetic to industry problems than to citizen complaints. Yet, admitting all this, it is doubtful that this fate is peculiar to the administrative agencies. It would appear to be part of the "life cycle" of all government, part of the broader problem of mobilizing energies adequate for our political purposes. Americans are a dynamic political people as is attested by the Revolution, the Square Deal, the Fair Deal, the New Deal. But perhaps more than is true, for example, of the English, we tend to move by fits and starts.

At this point it should be mentioned that some of the administrative agencies, though appointed by the President, are by statute "independent" of his control. In such cases the President cannot remove a commissioner as he could a cabinet officer with whose decisions or policies he disagrees. This independence is defended on the ground that where the agency's task is to make decisions affecting private rights, the necessary judicial attitude would be imperiled by presidential control. Critics of the agencies believe that this lack of presidential control tends to make them politically weak and ineffective. Since the President is not responsible for and cannot control their programs, they lack, it is said, the protection of his support and the dynamism of his office. They are easy prey to pressure from industry and from congressmen. Yet, it is not at all clear from the record that presidential officers are more immune from these pressures than the agencies, though no doubt a President prepared to make a fight can better protect himself and his officers than can a politically impotent agency. In my opinion, it *is* unwise to vest large policy powers in agencies for which the President is not responsible. The President should be in a position to coordinate their energies and their policies into his program. On the other hand, insofar as the agencies exercise judicialized powers, our strongly developed tradition demands independence. In such situations we must look to congressional control to remedy agency irresponsibility and inertia.

But these large questions of administrative organization are more in the realm of political theory and practice than of administrative law itself. The paramount concern of administrative law is the protection of the public and the citizen from the abuse of official power. This has been a concern of English and American law for hundreds of years. It has given us a body of doctrines enunciated by the courts, re-enforced by constitution and legislation.

These doctrines, however, are not static. The law is constantly being challenged to improve them and to adapt them to new situations. It is a general principle of our law that an individual's legal situation cannot be seriously impaired without a hearing in which all the evidence against him is presented so that, if possible, he can rebut it. Yet government employees, like employees of private industry, have usually in the past been hired and fired without hearing. It has been argued that a requirement of hearing and formal evidence would cripple management. But some change is taking place both in government and industry, as is evidenced by civil-service protection laws and labor-management arbitration. The issue has been acute in government discharges of alleged "subversives" and "security risks." The individual's employability may be seriously impaired by a charge which is in fact unfounded. Yet if the government must reveal all of its evidence, its enemies may be alerted and its sources of information dried up. The law has been trying to work out a solution which will give the employee a reasonably good chance to defend himself without requiring complete governmental disclosure in every case. Somewhat similar are the problems of hearing for a citizen denied a passport or an alien to be deported as a "subversive." In some of these cases we are making progress. But we have no cause for complacency. There is an unending struggle for just results in this field: the powerful must not be overprotected at the expense of the general interest; the weak must not be sacrificed to prejudice, hysteria or callous indifference.

X

⇒⇒⇒-⇒⇒⇒-⇒⇒≪≪-≪≪-≪≪

Archibald Cox

LABOR LAW IN THE
UNITED STATES

To UNDERSTAND our labor laws one must first understand the genius of our labor movement.

Until 1880 the United States was a nation of independent farmers, artisans and shopkeepers. Thereafter, the industrial revolution, the emergence of vast corporate aggregations of property, and the disappearance of the frontier converted us into a community of wage earners in which most men were dependent upon the sale of their labor for their daily bread and hope of self-advancement. These workers faced five problems:

(1) The individual worker was forced to labor at whatever wage the company offered. The corporate employer, who seldom needed the services of any particular man, could usually say, "Take the job on our terms. If you don't, there are others waiting."

(2) Job security became a major worry. If a factory dismissed its employees because of a lack of orders for

its products or if a mill dismantled its machinery and moved the business to another community, their employees faced poverty and privation.

(3) Industrial accidents and sickness, with the attendant loss of wages, were another source of hardship.

(4) Gathering thousands of employees into integrated factories concentrated vast power in the hands of the managers and their subordinates—a power all too easily exercised in arbitrary fashion.

(5) Men began to lose the pride of accomplishment which characterized the ancient artisanship. Reduced to routine tasks, they saw themselves becoming mere units of labor. They aspired to a voice in industrial decisions affecting them.

Every industrial society faces these problems. Some countries have tried to solve them by social legislation; their labor unions are essentially political organizations. Other countries have turned to some form of codetermination, to nationalization of industry, or even to violent revolutions.

Even in 1880 the United States was still a young country, peopled chiefly by men and women who had fled from government oppression. Life on the frontier also bred distrust of government and confidence in self-determination. The fluidity of American society prevented the growth of a class-conscious proletariat. The success of the American dream deterred radical reformers. American workers gradually turned, therefore, to self-help within the existing economic system. They formed labor unions in order to act as a group—to bargain collectively—in negotiating agreements with the employers establishing higher wages, shorter hours, and improved conditions of employment. If an employer refused, the union would strike until he capitulated or a compromise was effected.

Organizing the unorganized became the union worker's creed. The strike, the boycott and the picket line were his primary weapons. Unionization and collective bargaining would have little value without the right to use these economic weapons for, although negotiation carries its own compulsions, few "voluntary" agreements are executed in the absence of economic power.

Many employers bitterly opposed the unionization of employees. They threatened and discharged union members, circulated black lists of union organizers, hired labor spies and sometimes resorted to violence and intimidation. Gradually, however, the view gained support that the law should protect labor unions and encourage the spread of collective bargaining as a method by which workers might improve their lot without direct government regulation of the economy. This principle was put upon a permanent footing in the railroad industry by the Railway Labor Act of 1926. It was extended to all business enterprises (except very small local establishments) under the National Labor Relations Act of 1935, which is our basic labor legislation.

First, the National Labor Relations Act guarantees employees freedom to form, join and assist labor organizations. The Act prohibits specific anti-union practices by employers, such as discriminatory discharges and the establishment of company-dominated unions;

it also contains a general prohibition against any employer interference with freedom to organize and select bargaining representatives. Violations of the statute are called unfair labor practices.

Second, the National Labor Relations Act imposes upon every covered employer a legal duty to negotiate in good faith about wages, hours and other terms and conditions of employment with any labor union designated as their representative by a majority of his employees in an appropriate bargaining unit. The unit may be composed of all the employees of a particular company, of the employees in a single plant or a single department of a plant, or of employees belonging to a craft like machinists, carpenters or plumbers. Sometimes the unit includes the employees of several employers. If there is doubt about employees' choice, the representative is chosen in an election by secret ballot. Or the employees may vote not to have a union representative.

Thus our labor law carries over into labor-management relations the political principle of the majority rule. This is a distinct American development. The union which is designated as their representative by a majority of the employees speaks for all the employees. An employer is guilty of an unfair labor practice if he negotiates with any union except the majority representative or if he changes wages, hours, or conditions of employment without consulting the designated union.

Third, the National Labor Relations Act guarantees employees the right to engage in "concerted activities," by which we mean strikes, boycotts and picketing, whether used to support the union's demands upon an employer in collective bargaining or to aid in spreading union organization. It is this freedom to use economic weapons which enables unions to bargain effectively.

The tasks of preventing unfair labor practices, determining the appropriate bargaining unit, and holding elections to choose the bargaining representative are vested in the National Labor Relations Board, an administrative agency whose decisions are subject to limited review by the courts.

Collective bargaining goes far to satisfy a basic need of industrial workers—the natural, human desire to participate in decisions affecting their industrial lives. The workers in a plant usually elect the committee which, in consultation with paid union officials, formulates the proposals which the union will present to the employer. After a tentative agreement is negotiated, the workers may discuss it in the union meeting and vote on whether they will accept it or insist upon more favorable terms. If the employer and union cannot agree, there is a strike.

The National Labor Relations Act provides no governmental machinery for the adjustment of labor disputes. The only functions of law, it is thought, are (1) to protect the formation of unions, so that employees may exert sufficient bargaining power to solve the problems of workers in an industrial society; and (2) to provide the framework for negotiations between the employer and the employees most conducive to voluntary agreements. From this point forward the arrangement of wages and other terms and conditions of employment is a private, non-governmental responsibility.

I have emphasized the economic role of our labor unions and the legal framework within which conditions of employment are fixed by private agreement because this is the dominant characteristic of our system of industrial relations. But our labor laws also attempt to solve some problems by direct government regulation. The two methods are complementary. The statutes establish the minimum protection available to every industrial worker. The labor unions then negotiate higher standards by private agreement whenever they are able.

The interplay is illustrated by wage determination. The Fair Labor Standards Act establishes a minimum wage of $1.00 an hour for all workers employed in producing goods for interstate commerce. Special federal laws require contractors upon construction projects financed with government funds and manufacturers of goods under government contracts to pay the prevailing wage in the community as determined by the Secretary of Labor. These rates may be substantially higher than the $1.00 an hour required by the Fair Labor Standards Act. A manufacturer of electric-light bulbs, for example, must pay any employee who makes lamps for the government not less than $1.26 an hour. A contractor may be required to pay brick-layers $4.00 an hour.

The effective wage rates under collective bargaining are above the statutory minimums. The United Automobile Workers' contracts with the major automobile companies fix an absolute minimum of $2.14 an hour (plus cost-of-living increases). The lowest hourly rate in the United Steelworkers' contracts with the major steel companies is $2.03 an hour. The rates for skilled employees are much higher.

Hours of employment are regulated in much the same fashion. The Fair Labor Standards Act prohibits an employer subject to federal regulation from employing a worker more than forty hours a week unless he pays the worker for each overtime hour a wage equal to one and one half times his normal rate of pay. Collective bargaining agreements incorporate this rule but they also often guarantee double the normal rate of pay for any work done on Saturday or Sunday, and many call for annual paid vacations and at least eight holidays a year without loss of pay.

The way in which collective bargaining supplements the minimum statutory protection is most dramatically illustrated by recent developments in the field of social insurance. Under the Social Security Act of 1938 a retired worker more than sixty-five years old who has worked all his life receives $200 a month from the government. Many labor agreements supplement this government program by pensions financed by the employer. For example, a Ford Motor Company employee who retires January 1, 1961, after twenty years of service will receive an additional pension of $48 a month from the company. The principle has been extended by collective bargaining to life insurance, hospitalization, sickness and accident benefits.

The industrial worker's need for security against

loss of income due to lack of work is handled by unemployment insurance. Under the compulsion of a federal law each state maintains, by taxation and insurance, a fund from which weekly benefits are paid to workers who lose their jobs without fault. The level of payments varies from state to state, and also with the number of persons dependent upon the unemployed worker. A man with a wife and two children may receive $30 a week in Mississippi compared with $52 in Massachusetts. Some collective bargaining agreements, but only a minority, add to this. For example, under the contract between United Automobile Workers and Ford Motor Company an unemployed worker with five years' service is guaranteed sixty-five percent of his weekly wage for twenty-six weeks. This means that the lowest paid workers laid off after five years' service would receive $55 a week for the first twenty-six weeks of unemployment, partly from the State fund under the statute and partly from the employer.

Although a collective agreement is a contract enforceable in the civil courts, labor and management rely primarily upon private, non-governmental procedures for enforcing their rights under collective bargaining agreements. A grievance—that is to say, a claim that an employee's rights under a collective agreement have been violated—is usually taken up first between the union shop steward elected by the workers in his department and the foreman appointed by the management. If they disagree, the union's grievance committee, which is also elected, discusses the problem with the plant manager. From there the grievance may

go to a conference between officials of the international union and the company's chief executives.
Nearly all grievances are adjusted by this point. Nearly
all collective bargaining agreements also provide, however, that if a dispute arising during the term of the
contract is not settled in the grievance procedure, it
shall be submitted to an arbitrator for final and binding decision without strike or lockout. In a large company the arbitrator may be a permanent umpire chosen
by the parties who hears as many as several hundred
cases a year. At smaller concerns he is usually named
to hear a single grievance, either by the parties or by
some impartial agency. Most arbitrators come from
the universities, but a growing number have made arbitration a new profession. The awards cover a wide variety of subjects—the propriety of a discharge, seniority
standing, job classifications, piece rates on new products or operations, the computation of wages and even
such fundamental questions as the rights of the management to change shift schedules or install new machinery.

The handling of discharge cases epitomizes one of
the distinctive characteristics of our system of industrial relations. In some countries a worker who feels
that he has been unjustly discharged may take the case
to a labor court upon the ground that a legal right has
been violated. In the United States the law does not
deal with industrial discipline. Where there is a union,
the collective agreement usually prohibits discharge
without "just cause." An aggrieved worker may complain to the union that the employer has violated the

contract, and if the union can secure no redress from the employer, it may submit the question to arbitration before a private but impartial person.

Thus, the contracts and grievance procedures, including arbitration, provide an industrial jurisprudence with enforceable rights and remedies; yet it is done voluntarily by private agreement with little reliance upon the official legal system. The law provides the framework by protecting the formation of unions and requiring employers to bargain collectively. It recognizes the rights to strike, boycott and picket an employer's business. Beyond this, the conventional legal system is seldom brought into play unless the employer or the union refuses to perform the arbitration agreement or to carry out the award.

This system of collective bargaining, especially the principle of majority rule, gives the union designated as the exclusive representative wide power over the wages, working conditions and grievances of every employee in the bargaining unit. Under the protection of the National Labor Relations and Railway Labor Acts, unions grew rapidly in size and power. This combination of circumstances enormously increased the public interest in the proper conduct of the labor unions' internal affairs—in the handling of money in union treasuries, in the behavior of officers, in the admission and expulsion of members and in the rights of members to participate in the conduct of union business. Until 1959 these problems had been left to the courts of the forty-eight states without statutory regulation, but last September Congress enacted the Labor Management Reporting and Disclosure Act—a new statute regulating the relations between labor unions, their officers and members.

The new law requires labor unions to file accurate financial accounts with the federal government, which are to be open to both the members and the public. The theory is that the publicity will be a deterrent against misuse of union funds. The law also guarantees members the right to speak freely in union meetings, to sue the officers in the event of wrongdoing, to have a fair trial upon proper notice before expulsion from a union, and to vote in the selection of officers and upon other questions of policy coming before the organization. It regulates union elections in some detail, prescribing not only a secret ballot but also safeguards designed to insure equality among candidates and an honest count of the votes.

Since these regulations are new, we cannot be sure of their consequences. The hope of their sponsors is that they will protect the members and preserve democracy within the unions without interfering with self-government or curtailing their power to bargain effectively.

In conclusion, I would like to return to the subject of strikes, boycotts and picketing. It is essentially true to say, as I remarked earlier, that our labor law recognizes the right of labor unions to resort to strikes, boycotts and picketing; but there are some restrictions. Since the labor movement objects to any restrictions and employers often seek new restrictions, this is a very controversial branch of labor law.

The Taft-Hartley Act of 1947 outlaws a few specific kinds of concerted action—secondary boycotts, jurisdictional strikes and mass picketing, and other forms of violence in labor disputes. The Labor-Management Reporting and Disclosure Act of 1959 forbids the use of picket lines under some circumstances to induce employees to join, or an employer to recognize or bargain with, a labor union. These laws curtail the right of very strong unions to use their economic power in organizing workers, but they leave American workers free to strike against an employer whenever the union representatives are unable to negotiate a satisfactory collective-bargaining agreement. It is this freedom to strike which makes collective bargaining operate.

Because of the human and economic costs of strikes, labor law is concerned with the establishment of procedures conducive to peaceful settlements. The Railway Labor Act provides that disputes over new contracts involving railroads or airlines, which cannot be settled between employers and the union representatives of the employees, are to be submitted to mediation by a government agency. If the mediators cannot persuade the parties to agree, they must propose arbitration. If either party is unwilling to arbitrate, the dispute is referred to the President, who may appoint an Emergency Board to make findings of fact and recommendations for the settlement of the dispute. Until the Emergency Board has made its report and for thirty days thereafter, a strike or change in the conditions of employment is prohibited. The law then leaves the employers free to put into effect whatever conditions of employment they deem proper, and the unions free to strike.

There is no similar provision for industries other than railroads and airlines. If a dispute threatens the national health or safety, as did the great steel strike in 1959, the Taft-Hartley Act authorizes the President to obtain a court order forbidding the employees to strike for eighty days. Under all other circumstances the strike may begin upon the termination of any previous collective-bargaining agreement.

This method of fixing wages and conditions of employment carries substantial costs in terms of lost wages and diminished production. Sometimes the hardships spread to other portions of the community. The recent steel strike gave rise to many proposals for compulsory settlement of labor disputes. In recent years there has also been grave concern lest the agreements negotiated by labor and management endanger the public interest by contributing to inflation. During the next decade the United States will be much concerned with these problems, but although the government may play a more active part in the bargaining, it is unlikely that we shall substitute law for voluntary agreements. Most of us look upon the unavoidable costs as the price of freedom. We are convinced that negotiation of contracts is more flexible and more creative, and evokes nobler human qualities, than government regulation.

XI

Louis Loss

BUSINESS ENTERPRISE
AND THE LAW

BUSINESS ENTERPRISE in the United States is so largely corporate enterprise that for present purposes the two can be considered almost synonymous. Of course, there are many individual proprietors—the owner of the corner grocery store or pastry shop, the tailor or shoemaker, perhaps the real estate agent. And we also have a considerable number of partnerships—the French *sociétés en nom collectif*, the German *offene Handelsgesellschaften*—especially in the case of lawyers and certain other professional people who are not permitted to incorporate. But, more likely than not, even the delicatessen or gasoline station or drug store will be incorporated. And it goes without saying that the larger business units are invariably corporations (*sociétés anonymes* or *Aktiengesellschaften*).

The modern corporation has a number of characteristics which have made it the ideal device for investment by members of the public wherever free enterprise is recognized on this globe. It may be organized in a variety of ways, as the needs of the particular case require. An investor who wants to transfer his savings from one company or industry to another can do so at very low cost, and usually in a matter of minutes through the well-developed mechanism of the stock exchanges and the other securities markets. At the same time, the investor has none of the responsibility for day-to-day management. And the corporation as a legal unit survives the death of all its owners. These advantages benefit all concerned—management, investors and the economy in general—by channeling the citizens' savings into the financing of the nation's industry.

Moreover, the smallest family business may incorporate just as freely as the largest steel manufacturer. And the shareholder's limited liability—the fact that the most he can lose is what he has invested in the particular corporation—appeals to the businessman who wants to manage his own enterprise, just as it does to the small investor in a large corporation. Accordingly, it is not at all uncommon to find a family business incorporated, with father, mother and their children as the sole shareholders, directors and officers.

A corporation, in other words, may be anything from General Motors at one extreme to the incorporated "hot-dog" stand at the other. Both owe their existence to the state. Hence it is not surprising that they must organize and conduct themselves as the state requires. Just as obviously, the large, widely owned corporation needs more regulation in the public interest than the closely held corporation, precisely because the existence of thousands of stockholders produces a separation of ownership of the business from its managerial control. These differences between the elephants and the mice of the corporate world are recognized by our law. But it must always be remembered that the United States is a federation of states which have yielded only a portion of their sovereignty to the national government. And the line between state and federal regulation of our corporations has been determined by our political and economic history.

Basically and traditionally, corporation law is state law. It is now quite clear, as a matter of constitutional law, that Congress could require federal charters for businesses which want to engage in interstate or foreign commerce in corporate form. But except in a few special instances like national banks—which compete with state-chartered banks—Congress has never provided for federal incorporation. Consequently there is a separate body of corporation law in each of the fifty-two American jurisdictions: the fifty states, the District of Columbia, and the Commonwealth of Puerto Rico. Historically all this state law is part of the common law which we inherited from England and which the courts of both countries have been continually developing. But the state legislatures have systematized and developed the corporation law, so that today the law under which our corporations are organized and operated is for the most part statutory.

The basic patterns of the statutes are much the same throughout the country. Ownership of the corporation is represented by shares of stock, of which there may be various classes with different voting and dividend rights. And the corporation may also borrow money, issuing transferable bonds to represent the debt. Bondholders, being creditors rather than owners of the corporation, have an absolute right to their interest and eventual repayment of the debt. The stockholders must yield to the bondholders if the corporation fails. On the other hand, the stockholders have everything that is left after payment of the debt if the corporation succeeds. Hence stocks and bonds appeal to different types of investors.

The ultimate managerial responsibility rests with the directors, who meet at frequent intervals. The day-to-day operation of the business is conducted under their general supervision by the officers, who are generally appointed by the directors and are often directors themselves. The great function of the stockholders is to elect the directors, although a vote of stockholders (sometimes as much as a two-thirds majority in number of shares) is necessary for certain extraordinary events like charter amendments or mergers with other corporations.

It is also true everywhere that the directors have a fiduciary responsibility to the corporation. That is to say, they must act for its benefit, not their own. If, for example, a director makes a contract with his corporation and such a contract is challenged in court, the director usually has the burden of proving that the contract is fair to the corporation. Again, we have everywhere the concept of the shareholder's derivative suit. This permits any minority shareholder to bring a suit in the corporation's name against directors who may be enriching themselves or their friends at the expense of the corporation which they control.

On the other hand, there are many differences from state to state. These concern such important aspects of corporation law as the manner of voting, the distribution of powers between directors and shareholders, the circumstances under which dividends may be declared, and the rules governing shareholders' suits.

Under our federal system a company incorporated in the state of New York is a foreign corporation when it does business in California, just as a company incorporated in Canada or England would be if it were to do business in California. But in practice all the states permit foreign corporations to do business within their borders if they qualify as foreign corporations with the state authorities and pay certain taxes. This migratory quality has inevitably resulted in some competition among the states for the business of chartering corporations. Today there is no longer much occasion for an essentially local business to be incorporated in another state. But a disproportionate number of the larger companies are incorporated in Delaware—a small, largely agricultural state on the east coast which early liberalized its corporation statute—or in Nevada, one of the far western states whose laws are lax also in other aspects of life on this imperfect planet, notably divorce and gambling.

Apart from the problems of management-shareholder relations, there are also the problems of protecting the corporation's creditors in the event of its insolvency. Here, because the United States Constitution specifically authorizes Congress to legislate with respect to bankruptcy, the law is mostly federal. Our national bankruptcy statute covers not only corporate bankruptcy in the usual sense but also the complex law of corporate reorganization.

When an individual becomes bankrupt, any assets he has left after his personal exemptions are sold for the benefit of his creditors. He is then given a new start. The same thing is true when a corporation goes into bankruptcy. But, if the corporation happens to own a large railroad, there will obviously be nobody to bid for the assets except another railroad corporation. And so, in substance, what happens is that the bankrupt corporation is permitted to reorganize—to become in effect a new corporation—without going through the process of a sale of assets for the benefit of creditors. The corporation's debts may be scaled down or extended, and its capital structure may be changed. Through this process, which is available to small as well as large corporations, the corporation, like the individual, is able to start fresh. As a result, its creditors and shareholders probably suffer less than they would if the corporation were legally put to death.

There is still another special area of American corporation law, which has to do with regulation of the sale of securities—that is to say, stocks and bonds. This type of regulation began at the state level in the early years of this century, and today each of the fifty states except Delaware and Nevada has a so-called "blue sky law." This picturesque term became a part of the American language long before the space age. The state statutes on securities are called "blue sky laws" because it was once said that a certain type of promoter would not hesitate to sell property in the blue sky itself. These statutes are quite diverse in their details, but most of them combine three regulatory philosophies.

Under the antifraud philosophy, the state attorney general or some other official is given broad authority to investigate possible frauds, and it is his duty not merely to prosecute criminally but also to obtain court orders enjoining persons who have been guilty of certain practices from engaging further in the securities business. The second regulatory approach requires the licensing of brokers and dealers and their salesmen. And the third approach requires the registration of securities themselves, under various statutory standards, before they may be offered for sale. Some of these statutes, such as California's, go so far as to condition the right to sell securities upon a finding by a state official that the terms of the issue and the company's proposed plan of business are "fair, just, and equitable" and that the company "intends to transact its business fairly and honestly."

Yet all of these state blue sky laws were unable to prevent the stock market crash of 1929. A Senate investigation revealed the existence of price manipulation and other evils which prevented the securities markets from properly performing their economic functions. The problem was clearly a national one. And in 1933, at the depth of the great economic depression and shortly after the election of President Franklin D. Roosevelt, Congress passed a federal securities law. This statute does not replace the state blue sky laws. Congress might have gone even further if the state laws had not been on the books. As it is, the federal statute follows the less paternalistic philosophy of the English Companies Act in the matter of protecting investors. That philosophy is one of disclosure. Louis Brandeis, one of our great Supreme Court justices of a generation ago, reminded us that sunlight is the best of disinfectants and electric light the most efficient policeman. That is essentially the tradition of the Securities Act of 1933.

The Securities and Exchange Commission—an independent, bipartisan agency of the federal government which administers that statute—has no power to decide which securities may be offered to the public. But its lawyers, accountants, financial experts and engineers carefully examine every registration for a public offering in order to make certain that all the material information about the enterprise is accurately disclosed. This includes detailed financial statements which must be certified by independent accountants. In addition, the most essential portion of the information on file in Washington must be given to every investor in the form of a printed brochure called a prospectus. And, if the information is incomplete or misleading, the investor who suffers a loss may recover damages not only from the corporation but also from its directors and officers individually, the underwriters who distributed the security, and any accountants, engineers or other experts who cannot prove that they were reasonably careful. Hence the 1933 statute is sometimes called the "truth in securities act."

By 1940 the original Securities Act of 1933 had been supplemented by five other statutes which are administered by the same agency. Among other things, these statutes regulate the stock exchanges, brokers and dealers who trade in securities off the exchanges, investment advisers, certain electric and gas corporations, and so-called investment companies. These are not primarily corporation statutes in the usual sense; but they have had a great impact on the law affecting the large, widely owned corporations.

A company which wants to list its securities for trading on one of the stock exchanges must file periodic reports, again including certified financial statements. And, when the management or any other person solicits authorizations to represent holders of listed shares at an annual or special meeting of shareholders, certain information must be given to the shareholders so that they will be able to make an intelligent decision on how to vote.

Furthermore, when any director or officer, or any person who holds as much as ten percent of any class of listed shares, buys or sells any shares of his company, he must promptly file a report with the Commission. The contents of these reports are published. And, if any such "insider" makes a profit from trading in his company's securities within a period of less than six months, that profit must be paid over to the company. These provisions are designed to prevent corporate "insiders" from lining their pockets through their personal use of corporate information which is not yet known by the shareholders.

It is interesting that in Cuba—which in 1959 adopted a Securities Market Law modeled largely on the federal statutes in the United States, complete with a Securities and Exchange Commission of its own— even the revolutionary government did not go nearly so far in this respect as the Congress of the United States had gone a quarter of a century earlier. Under the Cuban statute the corporate "insider" who profits from buying and selling within less than six months is not accountable unless there is proof that he improperly used internal information which came to him as a result of his advantageous position. Under our statute no such proof is necessary. The insider's profit belongs to his company. It is as simple as that.

All this is federal law. With that non-doctrinaire approach which we like to think characterizes governmental control of the economy in the United States— an approach which is sometimes illogical but generally quite pragmatic—we have managed to use federal law in order to achieve a considerable amount of reform. And we have done so without creating an unnecessary concentration of governmental power which might result from a federal incorporation requirement. It is also fair to say that, partly under the influence of this federal legislation, the state courts and the business community generally are coming increasingly to think of corporate managements as having an obligation not merely to earn profits for their shareholders but also to serve the interests of their workers, their consumers and the community at large. Our philosophy in this respect has not yet been as clearly formulated as was the economic philosophy which served an earlier capitalist era. But gradually, as some scholars with a gift of poetry have observed, that amazing entity which is the modern corporation seems to be developing something like a soul.

A description of the law relating to business enterprise in the United States would not be complete without brief mention of three other types of governmental controls.

First, certain types of businesses are subject to special regulation, both state and federal, because of the kinds of services they render and not because they are corporations. For example, with minor exceptions, our public utilities and our transportation and communication systems are privately owned. It must immediately be added that "privately owned" is hardly an adequate phrase to describe American Telephone and Telegraph Company, the largest of all these corporations, which is owned by almost two million shareholders. In any event, instead of government ownership of these industries, we have subjected them in most instances to stringent control of their rates and capital structures.

Almost every state has some sort of public-utility commission. And at the federal level there are four independent regulatory agencies in addition to the Securities and Exchange Commission—the much older Interstate Commerce Commission, dating from 1887, the Federal Power Commission, the Civil Aeronautics Board and the Federal Communications Commission. The industries regulated by these agencies are, as we say, "affected with a public interest." At this very moment something of a public debate is going on as to whether we are adequately policing the ethics of certain entertainment and advertising practices in our television networks, and additional federal legislation on this matter is quite possible.

Secondly, one of the unique contributions of the American legal system—a contribution which is gradually spreading to certain other countries—is our antitrust law. Under our two principal antitrust statutes of 1890 and 1914, the Federal Government attempts through court injunctions and criminal prosecutions to prevent any one company or group of companies from creating a monopoly, or unduly restraining trade. With few exceptions, for example, it is illegal for companies to agree to fix prices. And, apart from public enforcement, any person who has been damaged by a violation of the antitrust laws may bring his own lawsuit in the federal courts and recover three times the amount of his damages.

We have by no means solved all our problems in this complex area in which law and economics meet. Undoubtedly, the economy of the United States—especially its heavy industry—is highly concentrated. But there are reliable indications that the degree of concentration has not been increasing in the last two or three decades. And we like to think that our antitrust laws are to some extent responsible for the economic progress we have made under our system.

Finally, there is always the tax collector, even for entities as immortal as corporations. Apart from the corporate income taxes and other types of levies which exist in most states, the federal government imposes an income tax of thirty percent of every corporation's net profits up to $25,000 in any one year and fifty-two percent of all net profits over that amount. This means that "Uncle Sam" is in a sense a majority partner in all but the smallest American corporations. The federal income tax applies also to profits made by stockholders from selling their shares, except that these so-called capital gains, when they result from an investment lasting more than six months, are taxed at half of the ordinary rate applicable to the particular taxpayer, with a maximum rate of twenty-five percent. And we have what amounts to a double tax on corporate income, in the sense that the corporation must pay income taxes before it can distribute any dividends and its shareholders must then pay personal income taxes on substantially all the dividends they receive.

If one broad generalization may be derived from this brief summary of the American law of business enterprise, it is that generalization about the American economic system is itself dangerous. One adult out of eight in the United States owns shares in widely held corporations. In the short space of the last four years the total number of shareholders has increased from eight to twelve millions. In addition, there is hardly a citizen who does not have life or health insurance, or fire insurance on his house or accident insurance on his automobile. The large insurance companies thus have billions of assets which they invest largely in corporate securities. And the same thing is true of the rapidly growing old-age pension funds established by private industry to supplement the federal social security system. Hence all these millions of insurance policy holders and employees have an *indirect* interest in the nation's industry.

This unprecedented expansion of the ownership base of American industry, together with the new regulation of the past few decades and the developing sense of managerial responsibility, makes it necessary to re-examine the traditional concept of "private ownership" as applied to our large aggregations of capital. "Public" and "private" are polar terms. They have also become emotional terms. It is well, therefore, to remember that in our context they have become quite fuzzy. Moreover, at least one conclusion should be apparent from even a cursory review of business enterprise and the law in the United States: that it would be as fallacious to think of the American capitalist system of today in terms of Dickens' novels as it would be to think of the size of today's world in terms of the time it would have taken Dickens to circumnavigate it.

XII

>>>->>>->>X<<-<<<-<<

Robert Braucher

COMMERCIAL

TRANSACTIONS

IN AMERICAN LAW

LET ME START with some general observations which
may give a perspective to the intricacies of the American law of commercial transactions. First, American
law can only be understood if the complex relationship between our federal government and the states is
borne in mind. Second, American law, both state and
federal, is more and more to be found in legislative
codes rather than in judicial tradition; and in the law
of commercial transactions codification has been associated with the development of uniformity of laws
among the various states. Third, commercial transactions in the United States are subject to a vast body of
governmental controls designed to protect the citizen
and to insure fair and equal treatment. Finally, every

aspect of our commercial life is colored by the fact that we live in a credit system, which enables not only businessmen but also workmen and housewives to buy and to spend on the basis not only of the wealth they inherit and the income they have earned, but also on the basis of the confidence others have in their promises.

What do these general propositions mean in practice? Let me take the standard example of the sale of an automobile. Fifty years ago the standard example for the American teacher of commercial law was the sale of a horse, but changes in American life have brought changes in the law and in the way law is taught. John Smith buys a new car from a dealer. He trades in his old car, pays part of the price by giving a check, and agrees to pay the rest in monthly installments. The contract is turned over to a bank or finance company which pays the dealer the full price. John Smith takes the car and makes his monthly payments by check directly to the financial institution. Until John Smith makes his last payment, the contract says, the financial institution retains title to the car and has a security interest in the car.

Millions of such sales take place each year. Instead of a car we might use food as an example, or clothing, or furniture. Or we might speak of business equipment —buses, trucks, machinery, typewriters, steel products —or of lumber, minerals or other raw materials. Commercial transactions deal with the process by which goods move from farm, mine, forest, or sea, through various stages of manufacturing and marketing, to the men and women who use them. The process includes not only the sale and resale of goods but also the terms of credit, that is, the lending of money and the process of payment.

I put to one side commercial transactions in land. Some of what I shall say applies to land, but in America as elsewhere there is a basic distinction between movable property and immovable property. Land law is in some parts older, more conservative, than the rest of our law; it is also more local. Much of our local government law is the law of taxes on land and the law of town and city planning for the use of land.

The sale of goods, on the other hand, occurs in a national market. Commerce with foreign nations and among the several states is one of the main subjects of federal law. We have federal laws regulating shipping, railroads, interstate trucks and buses, and airlines; the banking system is regulated by a public agency called the Federal Reserve Board; farm products are stored in warehouses licensed by the federal government, and dealers in fruits and vegetables hold federal licenses. People who cannot pay their debts may become subject to the federal law of bankruptcy. And every businessman must constantly bear in mind the federal tax laws.

It may seem strange, therefore, that most of the American law of commercial transactions is state law, that is, the law of each of the fifty separate states. But it is true. Each state also has laws regulating railroads and other carriers; each state has its own banking laws and its own tax laws. And all these regulatory laws, both state and federal, are based on an underlying private commercial law, which is almost entirely state law.

By private commercial law I mean the law of commercial contracts or obligations and the law of movable property, the law which decides private quarrels—disputes between buyer and seller, between borrower and lender, between banker and customer. Historically, much of this state private law was English common law, developed through centuries of judicial decisions, often under the strong influence of "merchant law"— the *lex mercatoria* common to all European countries. With this common background, our state legislatures often copy each other's statutes, and our state courts often follow the decisions of courts of other states. So we can speak of "American" law. Lawyers in America often speak of a "majority view" on a particular question of law; they are counting the number of states in which that view is the law.

But today more and more of our law is statutory law, enacted by the legislature. There is a compilation of federal statutes called the United States Code, which is coherent, systematic and comprehensive. Most states now have similar compilations. These codes are largely based on tradition and experience, and are freely amended by the legislatures. Probably they are more progressive and plastic, on the whole, than the codes of European countries. They are certainly more detailed, and in some aspects more complete. They assume, however, the existence of a body of underlying concepts and principles of private law developed by the courts of the various states.

In the field of commercial transactions, codification

of private law has gone hand in hand with the unification of the laws of the various states. About 1890, seventy years ago, the American Bar Association set in motion a movement for uniform state laws. Each state appointed commissioners to meet in a National Conference and prepare drafts of uniform statutes, which would then be submitted to the legislatures of the various states. The commissioners had their greatest success in the field of commercial transactions; all of the states adopted their uniform act for checks and other negotiable instruments, their act on warehouse receipts and their act on the transfer of shares of stock in corporations. Most of the states adopted the act on the sale of goods.

In 1940, twenty years ago, the commissioners undertook to revise their commercial acts and to combine them into a new Uniform Commercial Code. After interruption by World War II a final draft was completed in 1952; that draft was subjected to intensive criticism for several years by hundreds of experts, and after comprehensive re-examination and revision, a new draft was published in 1956. Ten states have now enacted the Uniform Commercial Code as revised, and efforts to obtain enactment are going forward in the other states. The new code for the first time provides a comprehensive codification of the law under which movable property and intangible property can be used as security for a debt.

Let us illustrate the impact of this complex body of federal and state law, both public and private, with a specific example. First, assume that a cosmetics manufacturer in New York sells a bottle of hair dye to a wholesale drug house in Boston, Massachusetts; the wholesaler resells to a local retail drug store, which in turn sells to a lady consumer. The advertising of the hair dye must not be misleading, or the Federal Trade Commission may intervene. The bottle must have a proper label and adequate directions for use and must be safe for use, under regulations administered by the federal Food and Drug Administration. Another federal statute forbids the manufacturer to discriminate in price among his wholesale customers. Federal antitrust laws forbid competitors to agree to fix prices, but there is an exception under which state law may authorize the manufacturer and his wholesale customers to fix a retail price; Massachusetts law authorizes such agreements and binds the retailer to observe the prices so fixed. If the bottle is shipped by railroad, the freight rate and terms of shipment are regulated by the federal Interstate Commerce Commission. Profits are subject to the federal income tax, and the retail sale is subject to a federal excise tax.

State law duplicates federal law to some extent, although it must yield in case of conflict: there are New York and Massachusetts statutes regulating misleading advertising, the labeling of foods, drugs and cosmetics, and agreements for resale price maintenance, and there is a New York as well as a Massachusetts income tax. If the lady consumer or her daughter or guest is injured by a foreign substance in the hair dye, the common law of both New York and Massachusetts imposes tort liability in damages for negligence on the party at fault, or there may be absolute liability without fault for violation of one of the regulatory statutes. The Uniform Commercial Code, which is in force as Massachusetts law, provides for the contractual obligations at least of the Massachusetts parties; the contract between the New York manufacturer and the Boston wholesaler may be governed either by New York or by Massachusetts law. Under the code, each seller warrants to his buyer that the hair dye is fit for use, and the retailer's warranty extends to members of the buyer's family or to guests in her home. If the hair dye is not fit for use, and injury results, the consumer may recover damages from the retail seller. The retail seller may then recover damages from the wholesaler, and the wholesaler may recover from the manufacturer. In practice, the manufacturer often carries insurance against such liability, protecting not only the manufacturer but also the wholesaler and retailer against liability arising from claims of defect in the product.

The hair-dye illustration raises a problem of quality; it does not raise a credit problem. More valuable items, like the automobile I mentioned at the outset, are more likely to have important credit aspects. Let us turn back to the automobile case. Automobiles may also give rise to quality problems, but primarily we think of automobile sales as the biggest element in American consumer credit. Last year the total personal income of Americans, after taxes, added up to more than 300 billion dollars. Total consumer credit outstanding, other than mortgages on homes, was about 50 billion, or one-sixth of total income. Out of that 50 billion, about one-third or 15 billion dollars was credit extended for the purpose of buying automobiles. (Compare these figures with the 80-billion-dollar yearly budget of the United States government.)

When we speak of the law governing the sale of automobiles, we must again stress the importance of governmental controls. General Motors Corporation is the largest industrial corporation in America and, like the two other leading automobile manufacturers, is under the constant scrutiny of the federal officials responsible for enforcing the antitrust laws. There are federal and state excise taxes and income taxes on the profits. The Federal Trade Commission has issued rules on unfair practices in automobile sales; a federal statute protects automobile dealers against unfair cancellation of their arrangements with the manufacturer; and a recent federal statute requires that the manufacturer's suggested retail price be displayed on every new car offered for sale. Every state has detailed requirements as to automobile equipment in the interest of safety; state licenses are required for the car and for the driver; in some states insurance against liability to persons injured in accidents is compulsory; and, of course, the business of insurance is fully regulated by state law. To prevent theft many states require that the owner of a car obtain a certificate of ownership from a state official.

In this highly regulated setting, the buyer of a car makes his purchase pursuant to state law, which establishes a framework for the agreement between buyer and seller of an automobile just as it does in the case of a bottle of hair dye; but the car buyer usually agrees that the seller will not be responsible for damages beyond the cost of repairs if the car is defective. The law of every state also provides that the seller may retain an interest in the car to secure the unpaid portion of the price, that this "security interest" may be transferred, that the holder of the security interest may seize the car and sell it if the buyer fails to pay, and that the security interest, if properly created, is superior to the claims of other creditors of the buyer.

If the car buyer is a consumer, buying for his own personal, family or household use, Massachusetts and most other states have further laws regulating the terms of credit. Banks are fully regulated; any other company which engages in the sales finance business in Massachusetts must obtain a license as a sales finance company. The contract must be made in a prescribed form, designed to inform the buyer of its terms and of his rights and duties, and a copy signed by the seller must be delivered to the buyer. Numerous unfair practices are forbidden. Finally, the credit or finance charge is limited in amount: on a new car, for each hundred dollars to be paid in installments, the finance charge is limited in Massachusetts to eight dollars per year.

I have given two illustrations of retail sales. From the point of view of the buyer, the purchase of a bottle of hair dye or the purchase of an automobile is a fairly simple transaction; he may not be conscious of the complex bodies of law to which I have referred, and he ordinarily makes his purchase without professional legal advice. From the point of view of the seller, the transactions are more complex, but these are routine transactions, and sellers rapidly become expert in handling them without professional legal advice. But if we shift to the credit arrangements of the merchant, we have to deal with more complex problems, and banks and other lenders will sometimes insist that the transaction be supervised by a lawyer.

Let me illustrate with a fairly common type of transaction. A merchant has debts owed to him by his customers, which he calls his accounts receivable. He desires to borrow money from a bank and to transfer the accounts receivable to the bank as security for repayment of the loan. The customers will be paying their debts every day, but new debts will be arising as the merchant makes new sales. Under the Uniform Commercial Code the merchant can make a single agreement with the bank; the merchant will transfer all his accounts, both present and future, to the bank, and the bank will agree to advance money to the merchant as he needs it up to some percentage of the total accounts outstanding at any particular time.

Such assignments of accounts receivable are complex. Each account involves a sale of goods, with all the problems illustrated in my hair-dye and automobile examples. The sale may be a sale on credit, with a security interest reserved in the seller, as in my automobile example. In addition, the bank is concerned with the rights of the merchant's other creditors. Under the Uniform Commercial Code the bank must file a notice in a public office to warn other creditors. If the loan is not repaid, the merchant may become bankrupt, and there may be taxes owing to the federal and state governments. To be safe, the bank must not only comply with the Uniform Commercial Code but also must take account of the provisions of the federal bankruptcy act and the requirements of the tax laws relating to priority for the government. Those provisions are sufficiently complicated, and the amount of credit extended is often sufficiently large, so that review of the transaction by a lawyer is worth while.

If we turn to another aspect of banking, the payment of checks, we find that sheer volume has forced the development of routine procedures despite the complexity of the situation and the law. Most American debts are paid by check; in a year our banks handle more than three billion checks, amounting to more than a trillion dollars. A large bank in a big city may handle 100,000 checks in one day. These vast numbers have to be handled in great batches; more and more our banks are introducing automatic machinery to do the work.

Only a tiny fraction of the checks raises legal problems, but the problems can be very difficult. In general these legal problems are governed by uniform state laws, in Massachusetts and some other states by the Uniform Commercial Code. But the banks are either national banks chartered by the federal government or state banks chartered by the state. In either case they are regulated by both federal and state laws. Bank deposits are insured against failure of the bank by the Federal Deposit Insurance Corporation, a federal government agency. The Federal Reserve Board issues regulations on the collection of checks and on many other subjects. The banks take out insurance against some kinds of losses, such as losses resulting from forgery; large depositors often carry similar insurance. The insurance companies are regulated by state law, and rights on the insurance policies depend primarily on state law.

At this point it may be appropriate to say a few words on the relation between the uniform state laws of the United States and unification of law among the various countries of the world. More perhaps than in other legal fields, a general similarity is to be found throughout the world among laws relating to commercial transactions. But minor differences between the laws of different countries may become very important when the transaction breaks down, just as minor differences among the laws of our fifty states often become important in practice. In many countries checks are governed by a uniform law drawn up in Geneva, Switzerland, in 1930, and there have been a number of other similar efforts at international unification of commercial law. The United States has adopted many international conventions, particularly those relating to carriage of goods by sea and to international transportation by air. But as to checks, for example, our federal government has been reluctant to interfere, since the subject has traditionally been left to our states. And our states have not felt competent to carry on international negotiations. Today our National Conference of Commissioners on Uniform State Laws is beginning to take some part in international discussions, but there are many, many problems to be resolved before tangible results can be expected.

Let me close by saying again that governmental regulation affects nearly every American transaction. Our friends abroad are sometimes misled by our slogans of "free enterprise"; they need reminders that in practice laissez faire disappeared from America long ago. And yet there is truth in our slogans of "free enterprise." Our regulatory laws set up more-or-less objective and rational standards; they do not ordinarily give some public official a simple power to disapprove and forbid the transaction if he so wishes. Moreover, the regulatory laws do not directly control the distribution of goods and services; in time of war we have had rationing and price-fixing by government, but in peacetime our laws for the most part provide indirect controls, setting the framework for the market in which private parties make the critical decisions.

The credit structure is particularly delicate. Americans associate the credit system very closely with their ideal of a classless and progressive democratic society. The market itself has a democratic quality, taking account of strength of desire as well as numbers of people. People can vote their dollars strongly for the production of baby carriages by saving on food or furniture. Credit introduces a dynamic element, permitting future resources to be used in advance; it is credit that enables the man with new ideas to introduce them into a society which might otherwise become stagnant. Credit is also a source of instability, creating possibilities of inflation and depression. Our governments therefore take responsibility for maintaining sound credit institutions and a stable credit structure. But people expect the government to avoid direct controls which would interfere unduly with private decision-making.

The entire market and credit structure, of course, depends not only on the stability of law and government but also on the mutual trust and confidence of a large number of people most of whom are strangers to each other. This mutual trust under law, essential in many aspects of civilized living, is particularly important in both democracy and credit. For a complex industrial society, it provides the equivalent of the neighborly mutual self-help of the smaller community, sometimes called the brotherhood of man.

XIII

≫≫≫≫≫≫≪≪≪≪≪

W. Barton Leach

PROPERTY LAW

THE INSTITUTION of private property is one of the
foundations upon which the American way of life is
built. The founding fathers believed, and we continue
to believe, that the ability to own property and to trans-
mit it to our families gives each of us an incentive to
produce to the utmost of our abilities—and, in produc-
ing for ourselves, to produce for the common good.

But the term "private property" needs a good deal
of explaining, for government—federal, state or municipal—often intervenes in the public interest and either regulates how the private owner can use his property, or taxes him with reference to it, or even takes it
away entirely.

In American law schools we find it helpful to instruct
by the case method. So I will start this discussion by de-
scribing a typical American young man with a typical
family, having a typical job, and living in a typical
American community. Then we will consider property
law as it applies to him—what it permits him to do,

what it forbids him to do, and what demands government makes upon him.

Sam Jones is thirty-four years old, with a wife and two children. He works as assistant foreman for a company that makes a variety of household electric appliances—washing machines, electric irons, toasters and the like. He went to the public schools, as his children do now; but after graduating from high school at the age of eighteen he took technical courses in a night school to qualify for advancement to foreman. He earns $7500 per year; his wife does part-time secretarial work; and between them they are able to save about $1000 per year. Some of these savings go into a savings bank account; some go into life insurance, which is really savings in another form; and some go to buy shares of stock in Sam's company and other companies. He is one of the millions of small stockholders—minor capitalists, as you might describe them. The savings bank account draws interest at the rate of about 3½ percent and the shares of stock produce annual dividends which would average perhaps 5 percent of what Sam paid for the stock. And then, of course, the capital value of the stock will increase if the company is a sound one; but it will decrease if Sam has chosen his investments badly. So Sam gets additional income from his savings to add to his salary; and the interest and stock dividends will probably also be put to work by investment to produce cumulative benefits for Sam and his family.

I think it well to pause here to point out the public effects of Sam's small-capitalist activities. When Sam deposits money with a savings bank, he (with many other depositors) makes it possible for the bank to loan money to the government, or to a businessman to expand his production facilities, or to a man who wants to buy or build a house to live in. When he pays life-insurance premiums he assists in creating a large investment fund in the hands of the insurance company —for such purposes as the erection of a $150,000,000 commercial center which the Prudential Insurance Company is now building in my native city of Boston, Massachusetts. When he buys stock in a corporation he helps the corporation to build factories, buy machinery and employ men and women. In a word, each one of these small-capitalist enterprises, added to millions of other similar transactions, contributes to the growth of the economy and the improvement of the general standard of living. Each is an example of national benefit through private incentive.

At some time Sam Jones, who has been living in a rented house or apartment, will decide that he wants to own a house of his own—perhaps in one of the "dormitory suburbs" that are characteristic of American cities. He might buy a house that someone is now living in. But instead he decides to buy a small lot of land and build his own house, partly with his own labor since he is handy with tools. He finds the land he wants, discovers that he can buy it for $2000, and figures that he can build a house for $8000. Here he begins to run into problems of real estate law.

How does Sam know that the man from whom he is planning to buy the land is in fact the owner? At this point, if he is in my state of Massachusetts, he must employ a lawyer who will search the title for him in the public records—mainly in the Registry of Deeds (where copies of most documents affecting the title are to be found) or in the Registry of Probate (where the disposition of land which has been owned by a person at his or her death is shown). By examination of the documents relating to previous transfers of the land, the lawyer will discover any flaws in the present owner's title and any restrictions upon the use to which the land may be put. But if Sam is buying land in the state of New York, he would take out a policy of title insurance from an insurance company which would itself search the title. And if he were in Illinois or Florida, the procedure would be different again—because the land law is controlled by the individual states, not by the federal government. But each state, in its own way and according to its own statutes and customs, provides some means of allowing a person who buys land to be sure that he is getting a sound title.

After the owner's title has been approved Sam pays his $2000 and gets a deed to the land. This he records in the Registry of Deeds. He is now the owner.

Can Jones build any kind of house he likes? Almost certainly the answer is no. In the first place he must meet the rules laid down by zoning laws and municipal planning boards; these rules are designed so that, as cities and towns are developed, sensible zones for various activities—residence, education, recreation, commerce, light industry, heavy industry—are estab-

lished in accordance with the public need. Thus Sam
may find that he must not build within twenty feet of
the boundaries of his lot and that the garage for his
automobile must be a building separate from his house.
He will also discover that he must adhere to rules of
the municipal building code as to types of electrical
wiring (as a fire-prevention measure), plumbing pipes
and equipment (as a sanitary measure), and driveways
leading to the street (as a highway safety measure).
He may also discover that, at some time in the past
when the lots in this area were laid out, private restrictions were established by a previous owner—as, for
example, that no residence must be placed on the lot
which costs less than $6000; but Sam would have been
told about such a restriction by the lawyer or insurance
company which examined his title.

Sam has saved enough money to pay $2000 for the
land, but he has only another $3000 in savings; and,
quite wisely, he wants to keep $1000 in the bank to
meet any family emergency that may arise. So, in planning to build an $8000 house, he will need to borrow
$6000. So he talks with an officer of his savings bank
and applies for a loan of $6000, secured by a mortgage
on the land (and the house as it is built). Since the total value of the house and lot will be $10,000 when
the building is completed, a mortgage loan of $6000 is
justified; but, of course, the money will be paid out by
the bank only as the building progresses, for the bank's
security must always be substantially greater than
the money it has advanced as a loan. So the bank may
contract to advance $2000 when the foundations are

complete, another $2000 when the roof is on, and so
forth. Sam will have to pay interest at about 5 percent
per year on the money he has borrowed; he will have
to keep the property insured against fire for the joint
benefit of himself and the bank; and he will have to
make annual payments of principal on the loan until
it is paid off.

The bank's mortgage is recorded in the Registry of
Deeds where Sam's deed appears. So this Registry
shows Sam to be the owner, subject to the bank's
mortgage.

What if Sam fails to meet his obligations under the
mortgage? It is standard banking practice for the mort-
gagee (the bank) to be patient as to minor defaults,
provided it is convinced that the mortgagor (Sam) is
doing his best in good faith. But if the defaults persist,
then the bank will foreclose the mortgage—that is, have
the property sold, usually by a public official, and out of
the proceeds of the sale pay off the loan. If the property should sell for more than the amount due
the bank, the surplus would go to Sam.

Let us look at Sam's tax situation with reference to
this house and lot, his other property, and his income
—for in any family planning, taxes are bound to be an
important factor. Sam pays an income tax to the federal government; for a married man with two children
and a family income of about $8250 (his earnings, plus
his wife's earnings, plus some interest and dividends)
the federal income tax is about $900. This helps to sup-
port the federal government in all its activities, including national defense, aid to foreign nations, national

highways, crop price supports for farmers and so on. Sam also pays a state income tax, which in Massachusetts would be about $100, though some states have higher income tax rates, others lower and some none at all. These taxes go to support the state government in such enterprises as the judicial system, state roads, state highway police and the like.

As to the house and lot, Sam pays an annual property tax to the city or town. The rate of tax differs quite widely from one municipality to another—it can be as low as 2 percent or as high as 10 percent. This money is used chiefly for schools but also for municipal services such as the fire department and police department. Taking an average, we can assume that Sam's tax bill from the town would be about $600. But here it is important to point out that the federal-income-tax law provides that property taxes and mortgage interest can be deducted from income in computing the income tax. So, although Sam will pay $600 in property tax and, initially, $300 in mortgage interest, the fact that these items are deductible for income tax purposes makes this combined expense of $900 actually cost Sam considerably less. Indeed the deductibility of property taxes and mortgage interest is one of the incentives which cause people to buy their own homes rather than rent them from a property owner.

After Sam has built his house can he sell it? Of course he can; and he will probably want to do so in some years after his income has increased or if he moves to another city. Since real-estate values tend to increase over a period of years he will probably be able to sell the house and lot for more than he paid for it; if so, he will pay a capital gains tax of 25 percent of the profit to the federal government and about 8 percent to the state government. If he sells at a loss, however, this loss is not deductible from his income.

I have said that under some circumstances the government can take his property away from him. This is by a process known as "eminent domain" which is used where some government—federal, state or local—needs the property for some public project such as building a new highway or erecting a government building. This is expropriation; but our constitution requires that the owner be fully compensated. If Sam is not satisfied with what the governmental body offers him, he may take the matter to the courts and have the value of his property determined by a jury.

What happens to this property when Sam dies? This leads us to the law of wills and requires some discussion.

If a person dies without leaving a will, then the property he owns at death—real estate, personal property such as an automobile, stocks and bonds, and cash —is divided among his family in accordance with a formula which is fixed by statute of his state. In Sam's case, one-third of his property would pass to his widow and the other two-thirds would be divided among his surviving children (or if a child has died leaving children who survive Sam, then that group of grandchildren would receive the share their parent would have taken).

However, any person who is of sound mind can

leave a will directing the distribution of his property; and property owners usually leave wills. In most states a husband cannot by his will reduce the share his wife would receive if he had left no will; if he tries to, she can renounce whatever is given in her husband's will and take what she would have taken without a will. Actually, though, a husband can usually defeat this rule by making gifts to children or others during his lifetime; the protection of the widow is far from complete. And the law gives no protection against disinheritance to anyone other than the widow, including children. But, of course, most men who are husbands and fathers take great care to provide for the future of all members of their families.

Another way in which Sam Jones could handle the disposition of his property upon death is to have it transferred to himself and his wife by a form of concurrent tenancy (called tenancy by the entirety) which will cause the whole property to pass automatically to the survivor on the death of either. One advantage of this is that the survivor has the use of the property immediately when death occurs rather than having to wait some period while the decedent estate is being administered by a probate court. But on the whole, for various rather complicated reasons, a will is usually the best solution.

Upon death the tax collectors again appear, although for a man in Sam Jones's present modest circumstances the tax burden would be almost unnoticeable. The federal estate tax exempts $60,000 before any tax at all is payable; and Sam's estate is obviously less than that amount unless he has a most unusual amount of life insurance (which is included in Sam's estate for tax purposes). As to taxes payable to the state, there may be none at all (as in Nevada), and where the state levies a tax it may vary considerably in amount. In small estates such as Sam's the rates of tax on gifts to widow or children are very low indeed and with liberal exemptions.

Let us now leave Sam Jones with his rather elementary small-property problems and consider a man of greater wealth, because to such a man the law of wills and of estate taxation presents much more serious difficulties.

In a chapter of one of my books I deal with the estate of a hypothetical elderly businessman, one J. A. Thomas, who has managed to accumulate some $540,000 during his lifetime. The chapter is sixty-nine pages long, and the will which I recommend occupies some thirty printed pages. This gives some rough measure of the complexities involved. I will try to indicate briefly what some of these are.

Mr. Thomas has a wife, several children and grandchildren, a daughter-in-law whose husband was killed in the war, and an aged dependent sister. Furthermore, the amount of his estate is so large that a heavy tax burden will fall upon it—perhaps $125,000. How should he arrange his affairs so that his numerous family obligations will be met and unnecessary taxes not be paid either upon his death or upon the later deaths of other members of his family?

Usually he will be advised to leave his property to a

trustee who is experienced in the investment of substantial amounts of money (this may be a trust company or an individual) and then make provision for
his family by directions to the trustee as to what sums
to pay to various people from time to time. A very simple type of trust would direct the trustee to pay the income on the fund to Thomas's widow during her life
and then to divide the principal among his children
upon the widow's death. But there are difficulties with
this. The income of this trust, after income taxes, may
not be enough to support the widow, especially if
heavy medical expenses are incurred as she gets older;
so the trustee ought to be directed to use principal for
support of the widow as needed. Also, the aged sister
and the widowed daughter-in-law need help now; so
there must be some provision for taking care of them.
Finally, Thomas cannot tell what changes will take
place in the needs of the family in the future; a son
may be successful in his business or profession and
need no help, or a daughter may fall into great need
due to ill health or loss of her husband. Consequently, it is necessary for Thomas's trust to have a
considerable element of flexibility to meet these possible changes.

This is where the type of lawyer who is an expert
estate planner becomes most useful. He has had wide
experience in arranging the affairs of wealthy men and
women; he is familiar with the rules of law which limit
the duration of trusts—and I assure you they are intricate—and he is fully informed about the tax laws.

In the case of Mr. Thomas an experienced estate

planner would quickly recognize several things. First, that Thomas should make some gifts now while he is still living, partly to give to certain members of his family a present sense of security, and partly to avail himself of exemptions in the tax laws that apply to *inter vivos* gifts. Second, that Thomas's affairs should be so arranged that upon his death an amount of cash is available, either by life insurance or by a present sale of stocks and bonds which might not later have a ready market, to meet the large tax payments that will be required. Third, that the will should be so drafted that it meets the requirements of the so-called marital deduction, which is a provision of the federal estate-tax laws giving a preference to gifts to a widow. Fourth, that some one or more members of the family should be given discretion—called a power of appointment—as to when and to whom payments of income and principal are to be made in the future.

Thus, in working out the Thomas estate plan, it is likely that the lawyer will supervise the making of certain *inter vivos* gifts, the rearrangement of Thomas's life insurance, the sale of some of his stocks and bonds, and the preparation of a rather complex will setting up one or two family trusts.

Is this unduly complicated? Perhaps some might think so. I prefer to say that the process is *unavoidably* complicated where a person is trying to meet multiple family responsibilities during a period of twenty to forty years after his death, in the light of all the changes in circumstances that may occur during such an extended period. It should also be remembered that it is a principal task of the estate planner to see to it that, after the death of his client, lawsuits do not develop—either between persons benefited by the will, or between the estate and the government tax collectors—which would deplete the estate through the expenses of litigation and delay distribution to those who may be in need of support.

The property law of most states is based upon rules derived from the law of England. Many of its technical terms—life estate, remainder, reversion, the rule against perpetuities—are those of the older English law. But, on the initiative of lawyers in the legislatures and under the guidance of the judges, it is in a constant state of change to meet changing economic, social and political needs. Justice Oliver Wendell Holmes of the Supreme Court of the United States once said that in law a page of history is worth a volume of logic. But that was said in the nineteenth century when historical factors had a tendency to be dominant. At the present time it would be more accurate to say that often a page of economics, a page of sociology, and a page of political science is worth a volume of history. Notwithstanding many elements of continuity with the past, our property law has become pragmatic and functional in its application both to the small landowner like Sam Jones and to the successful businessman like J. A. Thomas. It reflects a continued process of balancing individual and social interests. By restricting governmental action largely, though not entirely, to indirect controls, such as taxation, zoning, and judicial supervision of trusts, our law has sought

to preserve the incentives of private ownership and to
avoid the risks of excessive governmental ownership
and operation, while protecting the major needs of the
community as a whole.

XIV

❯❯❯❯❯❯❯❯❮❮❮❮❮❮❮❮❮

Erwin N. Griswold

THE LEGAL PROFESSION

IN ANY COUNTRY, a competent and public-spirited legal profession can play an important role; and this is especially true in the United States. The work done by the courts cannot be carried out without the participation of lawyers. Under our adversary system of justice, lawyers who are advocates representing clients present their points of view as effectively as they can, and thus aid an impartial tribunal to reach a sound decision. Apart from litigation, lawyers perform indispensable services as advisors to business firms, to government agencies and to individuals and organizations of all kinds.

In all he does, the lawyer exercises a public calling. Indeed, Elihu Root, one of the greatest of our lawyers, referred to "the public profession of the law." The lawyer is a servant of the public as well as of his client in helping to prevent legal difficulties from arising, or to resolve them when they do arise. Although his work may relate to a specific matter of private concern to his client, its influence may be very great. As Justice Holmes once said, the ultimate function of the lawyer "is to establish, develop, or illuminate rules which are to govern the conduct of men for centuries; to set in motion principles and influences which shape the thought and action of generations who know not by whose command they move."

Of more than 200,000 practicing lawyers in the United States today, some are trial lawyers. That is, they spend most of their time in the presentation of cases before the courts. A considerable proportion of this work today has to do with automobile accidents, although there are many trials in other fields, such as commercial controversies, wills, family and marital problems, and so on. When a lawyer tries automobile cases or personal injury cases, he usually specializes in representing either plaintiffs or defendants. This is very likely not a desirable development, but it is the way things have worked out. In the United States, a lawyer gets his work directly from the clients. If a man begins to develop a reputation as a plaintiff's lawer, then it is likely that the work which comes to him will be from plaintiffs. Similarly, defendants are often represented by lawyers employed by the insurance companies which have agreed to indemnify them against liability. The lawyer may, as a practical matter, find himself on one side or the other without much choice on his part.

Although courtroom work is important, and involves a high degree of professional experience and skill, and is sometimes spectacular, it has come to represent only a small portion, perhaps one-fifth, of the work done by lawyers in the United States. A larger portion of the work is office work. Lawyers spend a great deal of their time in counseling and in planning, in helping their clients to arrange matters so that they will work effectively and avoid controversies, and in negotiations leading to the settlement and adjustment of controversies without the necessity for court proceedings. Most of this work is done quietly and behind the scenes.

Some of this work is quite highly specialized. One special field is that of labor law. Both companies and unions employ labor lawyers to advise them concerning the complex requirements of the law of labor-management relations. Labor lawyers are also often responsible, to a very considerable extent, for the conduct of negotiations which are necessary in working out union contracts and in settling labor disputes.

Another field in which many American lawyers specialize is that of taxation. In this, the situation in the United States is rather different from that in most other countries, where most of the tax work is done by accountants. A large amount of tax work is done by accountants in the United States as well, and properly so. But there is also a large field for lawyers, both in planning transactions so as to incur the minimum liability under the law, and in presenting arguments and carrying out negotiations with the Treasury Department when disputes do arise about clients' tax liability.

In addition to these areas, lawyers carry on the usual functions with respect to the transfer of real property, sometimes called conveyancing, and with respect to family settlements, wills and trusts, sometimes called estate planning.

Lawyers also carry a high responsibility for the proper enforcement of the criminal law. Some lawyers do this as public officials, in prosecutors' offices. Other lawyers represent individuals who have been charged with crime. The private practice of criminal law has not been attractive to most lawyers, for understandable reasons. It is to be hoped, though, that many more will go into this field. Not only will they perform an important public service, but they will get invaluable experience in the actual trial of cases.

Another large field of work for lawyers in the United States is in various forms of government service. In a country as large and complicated as the United States, government agencies must have skilled legal advice. Many lawyers are employed by the federal, state and local governments. In addition, lawyers are often appointed to administrative posts where, though they are not directly handling legal questions, their training in law can be of great benefit to them.

All of these fields are equally regarded as a part of a lawyer's work in the United States. He is a lawyer, whether he is in private practice, working for a business enterprise, or in government service.

Thus, the field of law practice is very wide. One of the attractions of a legal career to many persons is the variety of experiences which it brings. A man need not specialize unless he wishes, although the pressure to do so, especially in the larger cities, becomes increasingly great as our legal system continues to grow in complexity.

Although our legal system is largely derived from that of England, we have not followed the English practice in the organization of the legal profession. There is no formal division of the profession in the United States. We do not have barristers, or courtroom lawyers, on the one hand, and solicitors, or office lawyers, on the other. With us, any lawyer is free to engage in any sort of legal activity, and he may be in court one day and engaged in drafting legal papers the next. Indeed, the notion of the separation of the legal profession into different branches is so unknown in the United States that most American lawyers have difficulty in understanding the English or French systems. Of course there is a certain amount of specialization in the actual activities of many American lawyers, but they are accustomed to doing whatever they feel their clients need and they feel qualified to do, and they find it hard to see how any other arrangement can be entirely satisfactory either to the lawyer or to his client.

Perhaps two-thirds of American practicing lawyers practice alone, having their own offices. Sometimes two or three such lawyers may have offices together, sharing expenses but with no other formal association between them. Many lawyers, however, about one third of the total, practice in firms or partnerships. Usually, these have a small number of partners, perhaps four or five or six. Occasionally, though, especially in a few of the biggest cities, they are very large. A few law firms have as many as fifty partners and fifty employed lawyers, making a total of a hundred or more. These large firms do an enormous amount of legal work, and do it very competently. Sometimes they are facetiously known as "law factories." Although these large firms play an important part in the American legal profession, they are not typical. The overwhelming majority of American lawyers either practice alone or as members of fairly small firms.

Even when carried out through large firms, law practice remains an essentially individualistic activity. Like the doctor and the architect and the accountant, the lawyer's stock in trade is his time and ability, and he works closely with his clients. There are a few law firms which maintain branch offices in another city, such as Washington, or even in a European capital such as London or Paris. But this is rare, and apart from this, a lawyer's practice is usually confined to his own community. There are no great national law firms, as there are great national accounting firms. Lawyers are local in their practice even though the representation of a local client may take them to many other parts of the United States or even to countries abroad.

Since the United States is a very large and complicated country, the organization of lawyers is also rather involved. Lawyers are admitted to practice by the supreme courts of each of the states, and this admission entitles them to practice in that state only. We have nothing in the United States like the Inns of Court in England, which are essentially private societies, membership in which entitles a man to audience before the courts. Through the Inns of Court there is a close professional organization of the barristers in England, and it is relatively easy to enforce discipline among them. Nor do we have a Ministry of Justice or other department of government which controls the legal profession. In the United States, after a lawyer is admitted to practice by his supreme court, he generally can go his own way. In this situation, it has not been easy to develop and maintain a professional *esprit de corps*.

From very early times, there have been associations of lawyers, and for about a century they have been formalized into bar associations. In most states, however, the bar association remains an entirely voluntary body. No lawyer needs to belong to it unless he wishes to do so. One consequence has been that many of the state bar associations are not very effective groups. Over the past twenty-five years, a number of states have passed statutes, or adopted rules of court, establishing what are known as integrated bars. Under this system, every lawyer must belong to the state bar. The board of governors of the state bar holds a somewhat official position. In theory, an integrated state bar should be much more efficient than voluntary bar associations. In practice, it has not always worked out this way, perhaps because most of our states are quite large, the lawyers are scattered throughout the state, and they cannot, as a practical matter, work very closely together, even though they are all members of an integrated bar.

On a national basis, the great organization is the American Bar Association. This has now nearly 100,000 members, thus covering somewhat less than half of all of the lawyers in the country. The lawyers who are members of the American Bar Association tend to be the ones who have had the greater economic success. Perhaps because of this they also tend to have quite conservative views on public questions. Nevertheless, the American Bar Association is not only the greatest organization of American lawyers, it is also a very important one which does much good. Being so large, much of its work is done in sections, dealing with various topics, such as the Section of Administrative Law, the Section of Labor Law, the Section of Taxation, and so on. These sections provide for the exchange of information, and for the development of suggestions for the reform and amendment of the law in their respective areas, especially on various technical points which would not come to the notice of the ordinary citizen or legislator.

Reference should also be made to another group of bar associations in the various cities of the country. Nearly every city of any size has its local bar association, and many of these are very important and effective. They serve not only as centers for professional fellowship, and interchange, but they also maintain law libraries, and in many cases have active committees working on matters of law reform, judicial selection, and so on. Probably the most effective bar association in the United States is the Association of the Bar of the City of New York. This association has committees which deal not only with local problems, but also with matters of national concern, and has long made very effective contributions on these problems.

The American Bar Association, and the state bar

associations, have committees on professional ethics, and these have adopted canons of ethics for the guidance of lawyers in their practice. Where the association is a voluntary one, the canons of ethics are binding only upon members of the association. In some cases, the ethical precepts have been adopted by the state supreme courts, and in the case of integrated bars, the ethical rules may have statutory force. The bar associations have committees on grievances, to whom complaints about lawyers can be made. Many lawyers serve devotedly on these committees and work hard to maintain high standards in the profession. When these committees feel a lawyer has offended against sound practices, they may bring a disciplinary proceeding into the courts of the state, and this may lead to such sanctions as reprimand, suspension or disbarment. In a recent year in the United States, seventy-three lawyers were disbarred in all the states together. This is less than three one-hundredths of one percent of the total number of practicing lawyers in the country, and is, I think, a fairly good record.

It has not been the practice in the United States, in contrast to England and some other British countries, to have a client's guarantee fund which makes good losses sustained by clients through a lawyer's wrong-doing. In recent years, though, attention has often been directed to this matter, and a few states are now beginning to start such funds or are making moves in that direction. This seems to be a sound development. All lawyers will stand better with the community when it is made clear that, as a profession, they stand back of their fellow members in their dealings with their clients.

Lawyers are a part of the professional group in American society. As such, they have status with other professional people. Their incomes depend upon the amount and kind of work they have to do. The average income of all lawyers is not very high, and is well below the figure for the average income of doctors. However, this can be misleading. Most lawyers who are active and reasonably successful make good livings, although they do not ordinarily become very rich.

Speaking in general terms, the income of lawyers varies with the size of the community in which they practice. The larger the city, the larger their incomes are likely to be. The income of lawyers also tends to vary according to the size of the association in which they practice. Solo practitioners receive the lowest annual incomes, while lawyers practicing in firms receive larger incomes. And the incomes tend to increase as the size of the firms increase. This may be in part because the larger firms are ordinarily found in the largest cities.

A lawyer's fees are largely a matter of personal arrangement between him and his client. In some communities, the bar associations prescribe minimum-fee schedules. For all matters of any consequence, however, the lawyer makes his charge, and the client is expected to pay it if it is reasonable.

There is one aspect of our system of lawyers' fees which causes surprise to lawyers from most other countries, and that is our widespread use of so-called contingent fees. In most countries a lawyer is paid so much for a case, or so much a day for his time, regardless of the outcome of the case. In the United States, the practice of contingent fees is quite widely accepted, and most personal injury cases are handled on this basis. When there is a contingent fee arrangement, the lawyer receives nothing, or perhaps a very small fee, if he is unsuccessful. If he is successful, he receives a percentage of the recovery, sometimes a very substantial percentage. It is suggested that this is a bad practice, because it offers an inducement to the lawyer to present perjured evidence, and otherwise to act improperly in seeking to obtain a recovery. There are, no doubt, some abuses along this line. Speaking generally, though, I think that most American lawyers would agree that the contingent fee does not have this effect. On the other hand, it does provide a very real incentive for the lawyer, so that he works very hard for his client. It also makes it possible for the person of small or modest means to obtain a lawyer. Such a person would not be in a position to pay the fixed fee of a client under the English system, for example, but he is able to give the case to a lawyer if the lawyer is to receive payment only out of any recovery he is able to obtain.

Although lawyers make their living from private practice, for the most part, they also have an important public responsibility, and this is widely accepted by members of the profession. It is natural in the United States for lawyers to enter politics. In the Congress of the United States, more than sixty percent of the Congressmen and Senators are lawyers. Many of our presidents have been lawyers. Many governors of states, and members of state legislatures are lawyers. Thus, members of the legal profession carry a large part of the load of self-government in the United States.

One of the things which has made this possible is the ease with which a lawyer can transfer from private practice into a period of government service and then back to private practice again. This is not completely easy, and the individual may encounter many difficulties. Nevertheless, it is widely done, and ordinarily with less difficulty than might be feared. For this reason, lawyers are often summoned to perform emergency public services of one sort or another; and lawyers fill many appointive offices in federal, state and local governments. Because of this, it is a matter of first importance that lawyers should have a broad training and a wide outlook. They are often called upon to deal with very complicated facts in public matters and to organize arguments and present them effectively for consideration and decision. When the lawyer does this task well, it is a public contribution of the first order. On the other hand, when a lawyer is simply obstructive, when he takes too narrow a view, when he goes into public office but continues, in effect, to represent his private clients, he may present a serious hindrance to the sound development of public affairs. In general, lawyers are public-spirited and are interested in public affairs, on every level, and their contribution to American public and political life has been tremendous, probably greater than that in any other country.

Even in their private practice, lawyers make an important contribution. Though they seldom wield great economic power in their own right, lawyers are often influential in determining the way in which economic power is channeled and used. Most of the documents and plans used by businesses, large and small, are drafted by lawyers. Lawyers not only help the business-man to do what he wants to do, but they also often act as counselors and guides, and seek to persuade busi-nessmen to make decisions which will be sound from the long-range and public point of view.

The ordinary office lawyer plays a rather un-spectacular role in the public eye. Members of the pub-lic know little about what he is doing. For this reason, he is often unappreciated by the general run of people in the community. It is the tradition of his profession that he cannot advertise or talk about himself. It is the nature of his work that it is highly confidential and cannot be discussed with others. Thus, the lawyer is usually encountered by the ordinary citizen in a some-what unfortunate position. The lawyer is seeking to enforce a claim, or he is cross-examining the citizen as a witness, or he comes in at a time of trouble, such as death or divorce. It is not surprising, therefore, that he is not always highly regarded. The lawyer who him-self knows the usefulness of the work which he is per-forming must often accept that knowledge as its own reward. In addition, he can take satisfaction in the fact that he is a member of a great profession whose tradi-tions extend back for more than seven hundred years. The development of the profession in the United States has been different from that in other parts of the English-speaking world. We like to think that the organization of the profession is more efficient here than elsewhere. It seems certainly to be true that lawyers in the United States have a more important role, both as business advisors and as public servants, than in any other country.

As Dean Roscoe Pound has said, the term "profession" refers "to a group of men pursuing a learned art as a common calling in the spirit of a public service— no less a public service because it may incidentally be a means of livelihood." The lawyer in America is an expert in a complex legal system. He utilizes his knowledge as an officer of the court in a spirit of public service. Though the members of his profession are widely scattered throughout the country, and have no corporate unity, nevertheless, there is a bond among them. To a large extent, the strength of our business and social life as well as of our political system depends on the degree to which the legal profession lives up to its responsibilities.

XV

David F. Cavers

LEGAL EDUCATION
IN THE
UNITED STATES

WHAT DOES a young man do in the United States if he wants to become a lawyer? (I ask this question about a young *man* because, for every young *woman* who seeks to become a lawyer in America, there are about twenty-five men who wish to do so.) One hundred years ago, the young man who wanted to be a lawyer would probably have become a clerk to a practicing lawyer. He would have "read law," as the saying went, for several years in the lawyer's office. Today, however, the road to the legal profession—a much more difficult road—leads through the law schools. Before I speak of the experience of the young man who wants to become a lawyer, I shall describe briefly the law schools, to one of which he will go.

Of the approximately one hundred fifty law schools in the United States, more than three-fourths are parts of universities. The universities themselves are of several types. Some are maintained by the state governments; indeed, forty of these state universities have law schools, with law students drawn chiefly from residents of their own states, for whom they fix their charges at a very low level. However, a great state university like Michigan or California will attract law students from many more states than its own. Then there are municipal universities, some public, some private, which obtain their law students mostly from the cities in which the schools are located. Many of these schools offer evening as well as daytime courses. The majority of American university law schools are in privately endowed universities. Some of these, like Harvard, Yale, and Columbia Universities in the East, the University of Chicago in the Midwest, and Stanford University on the Pacific Coast, draw law students from all parts of the country. In that sense, they are truly national law schools.

All the university law schools tend to follow basically similar programs of instruction though their faculties are free to plan their own curricula as they think best. The degree of Bachelor of Laws is awarded after three years of study; four years are required for those who take evening courses. Thanks to the combined efforts of the professional society of American lawyers, the American Bar Association, and the Association of American Law Schools, certain basic standards governing such matters as requirements for admission to law study, the length of the law course, and the minimum size of a law faculty have been accepted by about four-fifths of American law schools. However, even the law schools approved by these associations differ greatly in the number of their full-time professors and of their students. These differences are reflected in law-school curricula; some schools can offer a much wider variety of subjects for study than can others.

Let us assume our aspiring law student wishes to enroll in the law school at Harvard University. Harvard is at once the oldest law school in the country and the largest, having 1600 students, about fifty full-time professors, and a million-volume law library. Since I am a member of its faculty, it is the law school that I can best describe, and so I am tempted to use it as an example of legal education in a leading American university.

Before our young man can be admitted to the Harvard Law School, he will first have had to obtain a college degree. This means that he will have finished sixteen years of formal education when he enters law school, eight of them in a primary or grammar school, four in a secondary or high school, and four in a college. He will usually be twenty-one or twenty-two years of age, older still if he has taken his military service first. At his college he will probably have obtained the degree of Bachelor of Arts or of Science, but he may have studied Business Administration or even Engineering. The law schools do not dictate what college degree an applicant for admission shall have taken.

If our applicant ranked high in his college work and

in an admissions test, he will be one of the 500 to 525 applicants whom the Harvard Law School admits to its first-year class. In mid-September he will come to Cambridge, Massachusetts, across the river from Boston, and find a room in one of the Law School dormitories or in a rooming house nearby. Perhaps he will eat his meals in the Law School Commons. Maybe he will join with friends from college in renting an apartment where they can live together and even cook some of their own meals.

All the first-year law students at Harvard must enroll in the same courses. Several of these are designed to develop in the student an understanding of the nature and workings of the common-law system which the American people have inherited from the English and have made their own. These common-law courses deal with the fundamental legal relationships: contracts, property, agency, civil responsibility. Criminal Law is also a first-year course, as is Civil Procedure.

The first year of law study is the most difficult of the three. For reasons I shall explain shortly, the methods of instruction and study used in law schools are unfamiliar to the student. Though the number of hours of class instruction is not large—fourteen each week— the student will have to spend two or three hours in class preparation and review for each hour of class attended. As the examinations at the end of the first year approach, the demands of reviewing increase. Students form study groups to discuss their notes and past examination questions. Tensions and anxieties mount. Students breathe, eat, drink and sleep law.

After a written examination lasting from two to four hours in each one of his courses, our young man will leave Cambridge early in June for three months or so of freedom from law study—but not always of freedom from anxiety. It will be mid-summer before he gets his course grades. He knows that high grades will open up opportunities both in the Law School and in practice. Low grades, on the other hand, will be a handicap. Twenty-five years ago about thirty percent of the first-year class at Harvard did so poorly that they were denied readmission—they "flunked out," as the students say. Now selectivity in admission has brought Harvard's failure rate down to about five percent.

If our student has stood near the top of his class, he may have achieved one of the posts for which only the top-ranking men are eligible. The twenty-five men who stand highest win places on the Board of Editors of the *Harvard Law Review*. I should say a word about this periodical, now in its seventy-fourth year. Distinguished legal scholars and lawyers write its leading articles, but it is edited entirely by law students, free from faculty control, and it includes much student writing. It is a surprising fact that this student periodical has come to be recognized as the profession's leading learned periodical. Moreover, most of the other leading American legal periodicals are law-school publications, edited by law students.

Other high-ranking students at Harvard are appointed to a student board which administers a system of practice court arguments in which all students take part. Still other honor students may become staff members of the Legal Aid Society which provides free legal service to the needy.

The work of the second-year courses, which our law student must carry in addition to duties such as these, is heavier in volume than the first year's work, but the second-year man has usually achieved self-confidence and a greater capacity to work effectively.

In the second year, the student takes courses dealing with the basic legal problems that arise from the activities of business: Commercial Law and Corporation Law, for example. He will also pursue the basic courses of Public Law: Constitutional Law, Administrative Law, and Taxation. Moreover, to give the student a better understanding of the complex problems of modern business in these days of high income taxes, a course in Accounting has been designed specially for lawyers. Finally, to give the student a broader perspective in viewing the law he is studying than he can get from courses focused on particular branches of law, he is required at Harvard to choose one course from a special group, each of which can give him a new angle of vision. These the faculty calls "perspective courses." They lie in such fields as Legal Philosophy, Legal History, and Comparative Law. Courses in the last category include the Civil Law System and a Comparison of Soviet and American Law. Another perspective course is United Nations Law.

The second-year examinations over, our student, if he has done well, may find summer employment in a law office in a big city. This will give him some helpful experience, a modest salary and an association that may lead to an offer of employment upon graduation.

My mention of salary reminds me that our law student appears to have had no economic worries. This, of course, is not the case, especially since about thirty percent of the students are married and quite a few of these have small children. Before I go on to describe the third year of law study, perhaps I should pause for a moment to talk about student financial problems. Some students, of course, have parents who can give their sons the $2500 or more needed to pay tuition and living expenses for a year at the Harvard Law School. But, for not a few parents, this is impossible. If they can cover a part of the cost, their sons may be able to earn enough during the summer and during the school year to make ends meet, perhaps aided by a student loan. Only a rather small fraction of all first-year students can obtain scholarships. However, after the first year at Harvard, unless a student has done very poorly in his first year's work, his financial problems can all be solved. To every second or third year student above the bottom group who seeks financial help, the law school will give a combination of scholarship aid and loans sufficient to meet any genuine financial need he may have. This program of financial aids for students has been made possible by the generosity of the school's past graduates who each year give the school nearly half a million dollars, most of which goes for this purpose.

Thus protected against economic hazards, our student enters his third and final year. He must choose his program from a wide variety of courses and seminars. He sees many more tempting courses than he can possibly take: courses in Corporation Finance, in Labor Law, in Antitrust Law, in Family Law, for example. If he is interested in International Legal Studies, he may wish to take one or more of the twenty courses and seminars which today Harvard offers in that growing field. Moreover, he is required to submit a paper to the faculty as well as to pass his final examinations. Usually he will write this paper for a seminar. In that seminar and in some of his advanced courses, he will come to know and work with post-graduate students doing advanced work. At the Harvard Law School there are about one hundred of these post-graduates. They include students from about thirty foreign countries.

During his third year, our student may have been interviewed by lawyers from some of the many law offices that send partners to Cambridge to persuade able law students to join their staffs upon graduation. If he has completed his military service or can do so in six months, as is often possible today, our young man may have agreed to take employment in one of these law offices. It may be in New York or Washington, in Chicago, Houston, St. Louis, or San Francisco—almost any city of size in the country. He may instead obtain a legal position in a government department: federal, state, or municipal. If his law-school record was a good one, he will be paid a starting salary sufficient to support himself and wife—perhaps $400 or $500 a month. To be sure, this is more than many law-school graduates are able even today to earn at the start of their careers. However, whether they take salaried positions with law firms or open law offices of their own, most young lawyers of ability are soon able to become self-supporting.

Before the young law graduate can represent clients, he must take one final required step in his professional education. He must pass the law examination set by the state in which he wishes to practice. This examination for admission to the bar calls for a more detailed knowledge of the rules of that state's law than he has learned in law school, and so he will take a short preparatory course offered by some local lawyers. Once he has passed the bar examination and also an investigation of his moral character, he will be admitted to practice in all the courts of the state without further training. Only five of the fifty states require a further period of clerkship.

The need for a final course to prepare for the state bar examination points up a distinctive problem in American legal education. Since, upon graduation, American law students may go to all parts of the nation to practice their profession, a law school cannot concentrate its teaching on the law of a single state. Consider the situaton of a national law school like Harvard. It is rather like that of a law school established, say, in Switzerland to offer an education in law to students coming from every European country with a legal system based on Roman law. Except for the fact that all our students speak one language, we face much the same problem as would confront that hypothetical European law school.

We have been aided in solving this problem by the use of the case method of law teaching, the distinctive feature of American legal education. The case method was first developed by a New York lawyer who was appointed Dean of the Harvard Law School in 1870 and who bore the improbable name of Christopher Columbus Langdell. Dean Langdell rebelled against the doctrinaire lecturing which was typical of the law schools of that day. He insisted that the decisions of the courts were the true materials of legal science in a common-law system. Accordingly, he decided to focus legal instruction upon judicial opinions. For his course in the law of contracts, he brought together in one volume a selection of the leading opinions of English and American courts in contracts cases, presenting these in a logical sequence that was to be followed in the classroom. Thus was born the first casebook.

By 1900, after years of steady growth, despite much debate, the tested merits of the case method had persuaded all the major schools in the United States to adopt it. Casebooks had been compiled in all the main fields of law study, even those in which statutory law predominated. Today the case method, enriched and diversified in many ways, is used in law schools throughout the country.

In case-method instruction, the law teacher seldom delivers formal lectures, even though he may have 150 or 200 students in his class. Instead, by asking probing questions and by posing a succession of problems, he directs his students in a close analysis of the judicial opinions assigned for the day's class. The teacher tries to stimulate a lively discussion among the students. The student taking part in this must have a firm grasp of the facts of each case and not only know the court's reasoning but be prepared to criticize it. He cannot accept the court's decision as necessarily authoritative, for the very next case he reads may be drawn from the law reports of another state which takes a squarely contrary position. Or the student may find himself comparing the different solutions which two state legislatures have found for the same problem. He must grow adept in analyzing, comparing, evaluating, and projecting the lines of judicial decision and legislation which have been developed in those fifty social laboratories, the states.

Out of this study—which is essentially comparative in character—the student can scarcely gain a precise knowledge of a single body of legal doctrine, except perhaps in some fields of federal law. He does learn the main rules and principles that the courts have been developing, but more valuable than this knowledge is the insight he gains into the way legal problems arise and the processes by which lawyers and courts and legislatures have been seeking to solve them. As his study continues, he learns to think like a lawyer, as we law teachers like to say. He learns how to work with legal source materials, constantly to relate legal doctrines to concrete facts and facts in turn to doctrine, to look beneath the doctrines to underlying issues of social policy or practical administration. As each of his courses has progressed, he has had to review the cases analyzed in class and his notes of each day's discussion.

From these materials, he endeavors to construct, for his own guidance, an orderly statement of the legal rules and principles in the course's field. The result may not be a very learned summary of law, but it is his own, the product of hard, independent thought. From the experience of making it, he has learned more than his professor could have taught him.

The young men who emerge from this process are usually tough-minded, skeptical, pragmatic and resourceful. They have come, even as law students, to see law as an instrument which is constantly reshaping the American society and economy. Since American judges, in writing opinions, tend to discuss the political, economic and social policies that bear upon their decisions, students who have made these opinions a principal basis of their work for three years naturally tend to think of the significance of particular legal rules and decisions in terms of policies. Without often having become interested in the formal systems of legal philosophy, most law students have, consciously or unconsciously, absorbed the basic ideas of sociological jurisprudence championed throughout his long career by Dean Roscoe Pound, for many years head of the law faculty at Harvard.

The emphasis that the case method of law teaching has been coming to place upon problem-solving, upon using legal knowledge in planning business and property transactions simplifies the transition of the law graduate from school to practice. In the great city law offices, partnerships which often include twenty, thirty or forty lawyers and employ as many more, the young law-school graduates are given responsibility rapidly. Within a few years, they are beginning to handle the intricate business and financial affairs of corporate clients.

In many nations, law students play a very active part in their countries' political life. Surprisingly, this is not true of the students at most American law schools, despite the emphasis on policy considerations in our law teaching and the fact that American lawyers are in the forefront of every political campaign. The legal profession sends more of its members to Congress and the state legislatures than does any other calling. However, burdened by the demands of their studies, law students with a flair for politics either suppress it until after graduation or try exercising it among their fellow students. I recall one of the latter among my own students when I was a law teacher at Duke University in North Carolina twenty-five years ago. He was a bright student and a hard worker, but he found time also to be elected president of his class and the student bar association. He gave promise of going further. In fact he did so. His name was Richard M. Nixon, and he is now Vice President of the United States.

Since in the United States judges are not chosen until middle age, law students have no chance upon graduation to begin careers in the judiciary, though a few able graduates may serve for a year or two as law clerks to distinguished judges. Other law students are attracted by the possibility of careers as law teachers. These men are seldom encouraged by the law faculties to prolong their law studies at this stage. Instead, they are urged to go into law practice or into government legal work. After five or so years of active experience in the legal profession, those men who combine an appetite for the academic life with outstanding academic records begin to receive invitations to junior positions on law faculties. To persuade them to continue as teachers, the law schools have to promote them rapidly and give them substantial teaching responsibilities. Older, more experienced practitioners are also occasionally invited to join law faculties but, more often, their law teaching is on a part-time basis, supplementing a school's full-time faculty.

The recruitment of law teachers from the ranks of successful young lawyers has been influential in keeping the programs of American law schools close to the work of the practicing profession. It has also created full-time law faculties which preserve a lively interest in the problems of the profession and of the nation. In addition to their contributions to legal scholarship in general, law professors have been among the most effective expositors and defenders of civil rights in the United States. They had an important hand in framing much of the reform legislation in New Deal days. They are often called from the schools to serve as advisors to federal and state governments.

The continuous outpouring of new laws and regulations which must be expected in a growing, ever-changing nation with fifty-one legislatures has meant that legal education in the United States cannot be confined to the 43,000 students in American law schools. In their effort to cope with the complex legal problems of maintaining freedom and order in a modern industrial democracy, the 200,000 attorneys in active practice have begun to call ever more insistently for special instructional programs for practicing lawyers in expanding new fields of law. These demands are being heeded, and new institutions for post-graduate instruction are being developed, often with law-school help. As the members of the American legal profession are discovering, professional education for the lawyer cannot cease with graduation from law school.

XVI

Milton Katz

INTERNATIONAL LAW

BY ITS NATURE, international law is a common concern of all states, a product of the legal culture, thought and experience of many different societies. The central concern of international law is the relations among states. It is the role of international law to establish a workable framework for intergovernmental relations, and to provide criteria and procedures for the settlement of international disputes which are, or can be made, justiciable.

"Justiciable" is a lawyer's word. It is used to describe disputes of a kind that can be resolved justly and peacefully through adjudication by impartial tribunals on the basis of commonly accepted legal principles. In any civilized society, there are an immense range and variety of disputes that are justiciable, and are effectively resolved by adjudication under law. In even the most highly civilized and law-abiding states, however, many disputes are generally recognized to be nonjusticiable. They must be resolved through factors and processes other than adjudication. A familiar example is the struggle for political authority and control which takes place at regular intervals within the United States, at the levels of the national, state and local governments. These struggles are resolved by elections, which are acknowledged contests of power. Law plays a part, but only in the sense that it sets limits within which the contest goes forward. Violence and fraud are prohibited by law, and law determines who may participate in the contest as candidate or voter. Within this framework, the outcome is left to the play of political, economic and social forces. Another illustration may be drawn from labor relations. Within limits set by law, disputes among employers and labor unions which cannot be settled through negotiation and agreement are left to be resolved by strikes.

Questions of justiciability are fundamental in any legal system. In international law, they are not only fundamental but conspicuous and insistent. How are we to determine whether and to what extent an international dispute may be justiciable? How far may the amenability of an international dispute to adjudication be affected by the way in which the issues are shaped? If an international dispute is not justiciable as a whole, may it nevertheless be practicable to select from that dispute elements which, if separately handled, are or can be made justiciable?

As the life of a legal system is measured, international law is still young. Its beginnings are usually traced to the middle of the sixteenth century or the early part of the seventeenth century in Europe. Until the nineteenth century, it was essentially a European, and largely a West European, development. Since the beginning of the nineteenth century, international law has had to grow and accommodate itself to a much vaster international society, comprehending the states of North and South America, Asia, Africa and Australia.

International law is partly customary and partly conventional. Customary international law is deemed to reflect a consensus among nations, revealed through common practice maintained long enough to become crystallized into law. Conventional international law is that part of international law which is established by convention or treaty.

Few of us are aware of how many and varied are the treaties among the modern states. The situation of the United States may be taken as one illustration. A simple listing, by title and date, of treaties binding the United States and in effect on January 1, 1959, fills a printed volume of two hundred seventy pages. The treaties involve relations of the United States with more than eighty different countries throughout the world. In subject matter, they vary from cultural relations with Afghanistan, to trade in cottonseed oil with Argentina, to economic cooperation with Burma, to an air transport agreement with Czechoslovakia, to educational exchange programs with India, to an agreement on agricultural commodities with Poland, to a general multilateral agreement on trade and tariffs among many states, to participation in the International Bank for Reconstruction and Development, to membership in the United Nations.

During the past half century, a special kind of treaty has assumed increasing importance. This is a multilateral treaty, among many nations, which establishes a continuing relationship and involves undertakings by the participant nations on a broad front. The most comprehensive of such multilateral treaties, and the most heavily charged with the problems and hopes of the contemporary world, is the Charter of the United Nations.

Under the United Nations Charter, sanctions are available against acts of aggression, breaches of the peace and threats to the peace, within prescribed limits and subject to the will of the member states to make the Charter effective. Under the inter-American treaty system centering in the Charter of the Organization of the American States, somewhat comparable sanctions are available against an armed attack involving any of the states of North and South America which participate in that system.

Apart from acts of aggression, breaches of the peace and threats to the peace, international law may be enforced against a state only with its consent. Its consent is required at two points, initially when a proceeding against it is begun in an international tribunal, and again when efforts are made to enforce a judgment rendered by such a tribunal. The consent must relate specifically to the particular proceeding and to the particular judgment, except in the case of the International Court of Justice, the principal, judicial organ of the United Nations. Under the United Nations Charter and the Statute of the International Court of Justice, a state may file a general acceptance of the compulsory jurisdiction of the International Court of Justice. Within prescribed limits and subject to the determination of the member states to make the Charter and the Statute effective, sanctions are available to enforce judgments of that Court.

The requirement of consent by a defendant state is a serious limitation upon the effectiveness of international law. Nevertheless, despite this shortcoming, the extensive record of international adjudication and compliance by states with the judgments of international tribunals demonstrates the reality of international law.

States and statesmen have sometimes tended to honor international law more through lip service than through action. This unfortunate fashion has not been limited to any country. It has been widespread. The government and lawyers of the United States have shared in it. Realism compels us to acknowledge these facts, and it would be silly to try to mask them under pretense. But it would be equally foolish, and dangerous, to allow this recognition of unfortunate facts to deteriorate into cynicism.

However coldly and realistically one may look at the facts of contemporary life, one can readily appreciate the importance of the United Nations and international law through the simple process of imagining how much more brutal and hopeless the world would appear without them. International law has played a vital role and continues to do so.

Let me cite a concrete illustration, which involves American behavior. May I ask you to recall the Suez crisis of 1956, arising from the seizure of the Suez Canal by Egypt, and the invasion of Egyptian territory by armed forces of the United Kingdom, France and Israel? At that time, the United States was linked to the United Kingdom and France in a defensive alliance under the North Atlantic Treaty; and this alliance was only one manifestation of a close working relationship rooted deep in the history of the United States, the United Kingdom and France. In consequence, the invasion of Egypt confronted the United States with a drastic choice: it must either support its historic friends and allies or insist on the enforcement of the United Nations Charter and international law. The government of the United States, with the support of the American people and the American legal profession, threw its weight on the side of the United Nations Charter and international law. In the outcome, the military power of the invading nations gave way before international law.

I have already pointed out that the American government and legal profession have on occasion shared with the governments and lawyers of many other states a tendency to say more about international law than they were willing to do. One example of this behavior involves the International Court of Justice. In accepting the compulsory jurisdiction of the International

213

Court of Justice, the United States excluded from its acceptance "disputes with regard to matters which are essentially within the domestic jurisdiction of the United States . . . *as determined by the United States*." * This was an unfortunate reservation. It would have been more in keeping with the spirit of international law and respect for the International Court of Justice to leave the determination of the scope of domestic jurisdiction to the International Court of Justice. Within the past year and a half, the Vice President of the United States and the Attorney General of the United States have publicly questioned this reservation and have recommended that the United States reconsider its position. In addition, important parts of the organized legal profession of the United States, as represented by the American Bar Association and various local bar associations, have also gone on record in favor of a more wholehearted acceptance of the jurisdiction of the International Court of Justice.

If the present qualified acceptance of the jurisdiction of the International Court is seen in the perspective of history, the widespread concern among Americans to widen the scope of acceptance becomes the more understandable. During the nineteenth and early twentieth centuries, the United States was a leader, both in word and in deed, in submitting international disputes to impartial arbitration. Since the Second World War, the United States has been a party to two cases before the International Court. One resolved a long-standing controversy between this country and

* Author's italics.

France over the rights of American citizens in Morocco. The other was an action by Switzerland for the recovery of assets which that country claims belongs to its nationals and the United States maintains were actually German. In addition, a conciliation commission—really a judicial tribunal—has dealt with a number of questions of law and of fact arising under the Italian Peace Treaty, to which the United States was a party. It is also worth noting that the United States has a substantial number of agreements with foreign countries which provide for the settlement of disputes by arbitration or other judicial means.

I should like to devote the remainder of this inquiry to an examination of certain key problems which lie ahead of us. These problems can best be discerned against the background of the United Nations Charter, especially paragraphs three and four of Article 2 and Article 51.

Under paragraphs three and four of Article 2 of the United Nations Charter, all members of the United Nations are bound to settle their international disputes by peaceful means, to act in such a manner that international peace and security and justice are not endangered, and to refrain in their international relations from the threat or use of force against any other state. To this solemn undertaking to refrain from the use of armed force, there is only one exception. Article 51 expressly reserves to members of the United Nations the right to use armed force in self-defense against an armed attack by another state. When the Charter was adopted in 1945, the world rejoiced to recognize how long a step forward these provisions represented in the evolution toward a world ordered through law. The development of weapons technology since 1945 has underscored their importance. In moving us forward, however, these provisions have brought into view another range of questions, which have not received adequate attention. They must be faced.

It is a commonplace of any society that the rights and interests of human beings can be impaired by means other than armed force. Men may injure their fellow men through theft or fraud; through conspiring to deprive them of a means of livelihood or any useful employment; through injury in highway accidents caused by the careless driving of vehicles; through breaches of solemn pledges upon which their fellow men have justifiably relied; through false testimony and defamation.

All civilized national legal systems furnish protection against such injuries, and provide redress for them when they occur. Only because the law provides a remedy against such injuries, is it possible—and just— for the law to prohibit individual citizens from using armed force to redress their grievances in situations of this kind. Like Article 51 of the United Nations Charter, civilized national legal systems recognize the right of a member of the community to use armed force in self-defense against armed attack. In civilized national legal systems, as under the United Nations Charter, the use of armed force is not permitted to a member of the community in any other connection. At this point, the pattern of similarity between municipal legal systems and the U.N. Charter comes to an end. Civilized national legal systems, as we have already remarked, provide remedies against other serious injuries which do not involve armed force. Except to a very limited degree, however, under international law in its present stage of development and the Charter of the United Nations as currently applied, comparable remedies are not provided against comparable injuries in the relations among states.

It is a commonplace of international relations that injuries are inflicted by means other than armed attack, just as corresponding injuries happen within the domestic life of national societies. States may and do injure other states by means not involving armed force. A state may engage in sustained and systematic defamation against another state, employing all the resources of modern communications. A state may break pledges upon which other states have been induced to rely to their serious detriment; it may engage in deception; it may deprive the nationals of another state of all means of livelihood and violate long-standing commitments to them; it may engage in economic boycotts, and use threats and intimidation to interfere with the trade of another state; it may harass the communications of another state; it may stir up internal trouble; it may trespass upon territory not its own. In the nineteenth century and the early part of the twentieth, if the injured state could find no peaceful means of redress, it could and sometimes would resort to war, or to other coercive measures such as a so-called pacific blockade or reprisals which, while falling technically short of war, were carried out in the shadow of armed force.

Under paragraphs three and four of Article 2 and Article 51 of the United Nations Charter, the resort to war has been prohibited, and rightly and wisely so. But, with very limited exceptions, neither the Charter of the United Nations, as presently construed and applied, nor any other aspect of contemporary international law, whether customary or conventional, provides other means of redress for such injuries. This is unjust. It is also impracticable, and in the long run cannot endure. Even within the domestic confines of a highly civilized community, if the remedies provided by the law of torts, property and contract and the criminal law should largely cease to be available, it would not be long before the citizenry would return to the practice of self-help. The experience of the American frontier as it moved west across the continent is relevant in this connection. If the prohibitions against the use of armed force are to be maintained, as they must, the area vacated by force must be filled by law. This is all plain enough, but it is no less true for being obvious; nor will its obviousness protect us against paying the price for a continued failure to come to grips with it. So we come to the heart of the matter. How are we to come to grips with it?

Under Article 13 of the United Nations Charter, the General Assembly is charged with responsibility, among other things, for "encouraging the progressive development of international law and its codification."

A beginning has been made, in the work of the International Law Commission, established pursuant to a resolution of the General Assembly as the principal instrument through which the Assembly seeks to carry out this responsibility. The Commission consists of twenty-one members of recognized competence in international law, drawn from as many different nations. The beginning is important, but it barely scratches the surface of the possibilities offered by Article 13 to imaginative and vigorous legal statesmanship.

Legal wisdom and imagination could also cultivate other possibilities. There are seeds of growth which lie within the potential sphere of the International Court of Justice. The Court could be strengthened by a wider acceptance of its jurisdiction, and more frequent resort to its processes. Possibly it could be supplemented by an appropriate system of subordinate international courts. Where existing substantive doctrines of international law appear inadequate to cope with particular problems, it may be possible to develop new doctrines that meet the need. At times, problems may arise which cannot be resolved through any substantive doctrine of international law, whether existing or newly developed. In such cases, it may nevertheless be possible to cut the problems to a manageable size and shape —or at least to reduce them to less intractable proportions—by the wise development and use of legal procedures. Through a sustained and resourceful effort along such lines by all of us, protection could be extended to states against injury from wrongful acts not involving armed force. The negation of force under paragraphs three and four of Article 2 and Article 51 of the United Nations Charter would thus be balanced by an affirmation of international law.

Consider the long history of the civil law of the countries of continental Europe, and of the Roman law upon which they drew; and the history of American law, and of the common law of England upon which American law drew. While these histories make us soberly aware of the limits of effective action through law, they reveal the potentialities of growth in the law, in its substance and in its procedures. They also bring out the immense importance of differences in degree; the realistic difference between a little better and a little worse, and between a little better still and a little worse still. One need not dream of a millennium to appreciate the significance of these differences. In the long perspective of the history of human society and law, such differences in degree emerge as crucial in their importance. This is perhaps the true measure of the potential contribution to international life which can be realized through the growth of international law.

XVII

Harold J. Berman

PHILOSOPHICAL

ASPECTS

OF AMERICAN LAW

IT WOULD BE foolish to talk of an "American" philosophy of law. Americans, like the people of every
country, have different and often conflicting philosophies of law. Moreover, the various legal philosophies
which coexist in America are closely related to various
legal philosophies which have found expression in other
countries. Thus in the United States, as elsewhere,
there are those who accept a so-called natural-law
theory, which finds the primary source and the primary
sanction of legal rules and decisions in reason and morality; there are others who accept a so-called positivist
theory, which distinguishes sharply between law and
morality, and views law as the creature ultimately of
political authority, the "will of the State"; still others

follow a historical jurisprudence, which explains law as a product of the historical development of a people's spirit and character; and there are many who have adopted modern variations of these traditional schools of legal thought—such as sociological jurisprudence, which interprets law as a balancing of various kinds of interests, a weighing of the social consequences of alternative policies, or so-called legal realism, which is skeptical of legal doctrine and which finds the source of legal decisions in the economic, psychological or ideological preferences of the decision-makers. Each of these legal philosophies has its advocates, and each has had its period of popularity at one time or another in our history.

Many Americans, on the other hand, distrust legal philosophy altogether. It is often said that American law, like English law, is highly empirical in its method, that it proceeds from case to case and from problem to problem, seeking practical solutions without reference to a systematic set of doctrines or a comprehensive theory. "The life of the law," said one of our most famous jurists, Oliver Wendell Holmes, Jr., "has not been logic but experience." Experience, many would say, and especially legal experience, "the life of the law," can only be understood in pragmatic terms: first one thing happens and then another, depending on a multiplicity of factors which are only superficially interconnected.

I would contend, however, that our distrust of philosophy is rather a distrust of particular philosophies, a fear that the vitality of our legal system will suffer if it is confined by a single theory. Our celebrated pragmatism may conceal the fact that we are actually choosing from various competing legal theories those truths which each is thought to contain.

This may be demonstrated if we examine the extent to which various theories of law are implicit in various American legal institutions and practices. I would contend that certain features of our law are based upon a belief in natural law; other features are based upon a theory of positivism; still others are based upon historical jurisprudence; still others upon other legal philosophies. In the abstract, these legal philosophies may be inconsistent with each other; in life, they are reconciled, and the truth is found in the right combination of them at the right time.

Let us consider, first, the belief that law is an expression of man's rational and moral nature and that any particular law must be interpreted in the light of the rational and moral purposes which it is designed to fulfill. This belief, which presupposes that what "is" cannot be divorced entirely from what "ought to be," and that a rule or command cannot properly be called law if it violates the ideals for which law itself exists, is disputed by many in America today; yet unquestionably it has exercised an important influence on American legal development, and, further, certain features of American law presuppose its validity.

In an earlier period of our history, especially in the late eighteenth and early nineteenth centuries, most of our leading jurists fully accepted the view that there is a "moral law," or a "higher law," by which legislatures, courts and administrative officials are bound and which is superior to statutes, precedents, or custom. Partly under the influence of European writers such as Grotius, Vattel, and Pufendorf, American judges in that era declared that legislation must be interpreted consistently with natural reason and natural justice, and they asserted the then quite radical doctrine that courts must refuse to give effect to statutes which they consider to be contrary to constitutional principles. Although the judicial power to annul unconstitutional acts of the legislature may perhaps be justified without resort to a theory of a "law of nature," it is nevertheless significant that the judges who first invoked that power did accept such a theory.

In this connection it must be stressed that the Constitution itself specifically enacts, as positive law, certain broad principles of moral justice. Thus the Constitution states that no person may be deprived of life, liberty or property without "due process of law"—a phrase which means to an American what the phrase "natural law" has meant traditionally, namely, equality, consistency, impartiality, justice, fairness. The Constitution also guarantees certain broad freedoms such as freedom of speech and of religion, and certain broad rights such as the right not to be subjected to unreasonable searches and seizures, the right to an impartial trial, and the right of all citizens to equal protection of the laws. By requiring that all laws must conform to these moral principles, the Constitution has encouraged American judges to submit to the test of conscience not only legislation, but all legal rules and all governmental acts, including their own judicial decisions. It would be wrong to infer from this that American judges feel free to decide a case without regard to statute, precedent and custom; on the contrary, stability of laws and consistency of decisions are basic values of our judicial system. Nevertheless it is of the greatest significance that the judge can at times say: a statute (or a rule, or an official act) which conflicts with justice is not law. He can do this when the Constitution is infringed; but the power of judicial review of the constitutionality of legislation has had a pervasive influence on the entire legal system, for lurking in the background of every case, civil or criminal or administrative, is the constitutional requirement of "due process of law." A gross injustice always suggests, at least, a constitutional issue.

Another aspect of American law which expresses a natural-law theory is the doctrine that the English common law as it existed prior to the American Revolution is applicable in the various states only insofar as it is suitable to our conditions. Reflected in this doctrine is a belief in an ideal common law which is capable of being adapted to the nature of our society. Thus to a certain extent, at least, common-law principles, like constitutional principles, are treated as a kind of law of nature—a natural law, one must add, which is conceived less in terms of Stoic and Thomist conceptions of man's natural inclination to do good and avoid evil than in terms of Calvinist conceptions of the diverse institutional arrangements required in order to keep man's sinful nature under control.

In considering the extent to which our legal institutions are influenced by a theory of natural law one must also take into account the high social and political status of our judges. The American judge comes to office typically after a successful career in legal practice, and often after some participation in politics; he is generally a well-known figure in public life. The title "Judge" is considered a title of special honor, and a person who has once been a judge will be referred to by that title even if he has resigned from the judiciary and has gone back to legal practice or perhaps to a high political post. The judiciary, with us, is not a civil service but an independent branch of government, coequal with the legislative and the executive. In addition, because our social order is a pluralistic one, in which many races and traditions and economic interests must be reconciled on a continental scale, political conflicts often cannot be resolved by legislation and instead become channeled into grooves of private litigation; the courts are therefore called upon to decide basic political questions which cannot be divorced from moral questions. Racial desegregation is a striking example of such a political and moral issue which has become a legal question to be decided by the courts; but there are less dramatic examples which come up every day. Shall schools and hospitals be immune from liability for personal injuries inflicted by their employees because they are charitable institutions? Shall gambling contracts be enforced? Is a particular book obscene and its sale therefore subject to prohibition? Hosts of such questions are litigated in the courts, either because the legislature has not attempted to give an answer to them or because the legislative enactment is subject to various interpretations. The high status of the judiciary, as well as the great significance of many of the issues which are presented for judicial decision, help to sustain the belief that the judge is not only an official of the state but that he is also subject to an authority higher than the state— that, in the words of the medieval English jurist Bracton, he is "not under man but under law and under God."

In the latter nineteenth and early twentieth centuries, the belief in a higher moral law by which judicial decisions must be guided was transformed into a belief in certain immutable natural rights, chiefly rights of private property and freedom of contract, which the courts of that era held to be implicit in the Constitution and hence superior to any legislation. In the name of such absolute private rights, the Supreme Court at that time annulled legislative efforts to regulate child labor, to establish minimum wages and maximum hours of work, and to enact other kinds of social welfare measures, including even the income tax. Although this doctrine of immutable natural rights was often confused with the earlier doctrine of the supremacy of the moral law, in fact the two were quite different. The natural-rights theory postulated the existence of fixed norms and concepts by which legal rules were to be judged, whereas the earlier theory spoke in terms of the conformity of legal rules to broader and more flexible standards of justice. Thus the natural-rights theory was associated with a desire for a higher degree of predictability of decision than the earlier natural-law theory seemed to provide. Indeed, it was in the heyday of the natural-rights theory—the theory that private rights of property and contract are sacred —that many of our courts adopted a strict doctrine of adherence to precedent, called *stare decisis*, under which they declared themselves bound by prior decisions, however unjust. *Stare decisis*, in turn, was associated with the idea that each judicial decision stands for a rule of law, and that from the body of legal rules conclusions can be drawn as a matter of syllogistic logic, regardless of social consequences.

And so a mechanical reasoning took a place alongside the earlier moral reasoning as a predominant characteristic of American legal thought. As has happened so often in the history of legal systems, an era of "equity" was followed by an era of "strict law." Accepting as axiomatic that "the law is the law," many of our courts and our jurists sought to construct a legal system which would be self-sufficient, complete, and impervious to fundamental change. Of course this quest for legal certainty was bound to fail, for law can never be isolated from economic, political and social change; and this period in American history—approximately from the end of the Civil War to the First World War—was an era of rapid industrialization, mass immigration from Europe, the building of our cities and enormous growth in all areas of social life. Nevertheless, here, as in nineteenth-century Europe, jurists conceived their primary task to be that of analysis, classification, and systematization.

Thus, paradoxically, the concept of fixed natural rights—although it imposed limitations upon the legislature—was congenial to a positivist philosophy of law, insofar as it stressed the self-containment and independence of the system of legal rules. In contrast with its European counterpart, American legal positivism has not laid such great stress upon the role of the state as the source of law—partly, perhaps, because the Machiavellian term "state" has never corresponded to American political realities. "State" has become confused in our political thought with "government"; and we tend to think of the political process not in unitary terms but as a complex interaction of political parties, public opinion, conflicting federal and state powers, and checks and balances among the legislative, executive, and judicial branches. Our positivist legal theory does, however, like its European counterpart, consider law as a body of rules to be applied logically and rationally to the facts of particular cases, regardless of justice in some abstract sense. Moral considerations are for the legislature, in this view, not for the court. As Justice Holmes once wrote in a letter to a friend: "I have said to my brethren [on the Supreme Court] many times that I hate justice, which means that I know if a man begins to talk about that, for one reason or another he is shirking thinking in legal terms." It was Holmes, indeed, who more than any other person influenced three generations of American jurists to accept a positivist theory; from 1882 to 1932, during twenty years on the Massachusetts Supreme Judicial Court and then thirty years on the United States Supreme Court, he fought against any confusion of law and morals, and in a series of brilliant dissenting opinions he propounded the doctrine that the economic and moral beliefs of the judges should not limit the right of the majority to enact its will into law.

Apart from its effect in narrowing the range of considerations relevant to the interpretation of legal rules, positivism's principal contribution to American law has consisted in the impetus which it has given to a systematization of our legal doctrine. Although we resisted a comprehensive codification of law in the European sense, the late nineteenth and early twentieth centuries were, for our law, a time of systematic formulation of legal norms and restatement of doctrine in particular fields. In the commercial field the basic concepts and rules of sales, of negotiable instruments, and of various types of credit were codified. In the field of tort law, the many various types of remedies for different kinds of injuries were subjected to rigorous analysis in order to derive their underlying principles and thus gradually to eliminate their inconsistencies. In civil procedure, the anachronisms of the older common-law rules were largely discarded, often by means of the adoption of new codes of procedure which simplified and rationalized the system of pleading and of trials and appeals. Other examples could be added to show the movement of our law, in that period and today, toward increased certainty and predictability. Of course these developments are consistent with various legal philosophies, but it is nevertheless significant that they took place largely within the framework of a positivist conception.

Although the struggle between positivist and natural-law conceptions has dominated American legal thinking—as it has dominated the legal thinking of many other countries—there have been other important intellectual developments which have also left their mark upon our legal institutions. Since the 1920's and 1930's American legal thought has tended to focus on the necessity for interpreting legal rules, and reaching legal decisions, in terms of the social consequences of those rules and decisions. Many have come to view law primarily as an instrument of social change, of "social engineering." The concept of a sociological jurisprudence, associated particularly with the writings of Roscoe Pound, has had a profound effect in freeing American law from the myth that legal concepts and rules can be viewed in isolation from their social context. Building in part on the work of the great nineteenth-century German jurist von Jhering, Pound attacked legal formalism and conceptualism and urged that legal doctrine be understood as a balancing of various kinds of individual and group interests—the limits of a reasonable adjustment being determined by the interests of society and by public policy.

Another school of thought, however, has gone beyond Pound, viewing legal realities not in terms of doctrine at all, but in terms of behavior, especially official behavior. Under the slogan of "legal realism," many

American jurists, especially in the 1930's, turned to economic, psychological and ideological factors in their search for the underlying causes which determine the behavior of judges, lawyers, and other official decision-makers. Building on Holmes, the legal realists have contended that so-called rules of law are simply generalized statements of what the behavior pattern of officials supposedly is, and that the source of that behavior pattern is to be found chiefly outside the law, in the policies, prejudices, and preferences of the officials.

The philosophies of sociological jurisprudence and legal realism played an important part in the great social and economic reforms of the 1930's which are associated with President Franklin Delano Roosevelt and the New Deal. These philosophies permitted the overthrow during that period of many established rules; what formerly was held sacred came to be seen as shibboleth. In addition these philosophies were congenial to the belief in administration as a better means of solving social problems than adjudication; as law came to be seen essentially as a means of social and economic regulation, the role of the administrator was enhanced, for he has more adequate means of investigating and regulating social conflict than the judge. At the same time the newer legal philosophies have had important effects on the judicial process as well, for the emphasis upon the social policies underlying legal rules and decisions has led to an expansion, once again, of the range of considerations appropriate for the argument and decision of cases.

The Second World War helped us to realize, however, the limitations of a legal philosophy which exaggerates the role of the political and administrative element in law. Our experience as a nation in arms taught us the difference between a system of command and a system of law; it also taught us the dangers of excessive administrative centralization. In addition, the war itself required the acceptance of values and symbols sacred enough to die for; and for that, the skepticism of the legal realists was not adequate. Finally, the exploitation of legal forms by the totalitarian regimes compelled us to re-examine the theory that law is ultimately the creature of political authority, for if there is no authority beyond that of the political rulers, whether they be dictators or popular majorities, then we cannot entirely blame those who blindly carried out Hitler's orders. At least they were "law abiding," in the positivist's sense.

Since the war we have witnessed, therefore, a revival of natural-law theories. Perhaps the most striking effect of this revival has been in the area of civil liberties, where jurists who formerly denounced the Supreme Court for imposing a "higher law" upon legislative and administrative policies in the sphere of social and economic welfare, have rallied to support the Court's defense of freedom of speech, racial equality, and procedural rights against legislative and administrative infringements.

In other fields as well—apart from constitutional law—there has been a renewed emphasis upon the rational purposes of legal concepts and legal institutions.

In contract law, for example, writers such as Professor Lon Fuller of Harvard and Professor Karl Llewellyn of Chicago—though taking different starting-points—have insisted that we ask what contract is *for*, and not merely what contract *is*. As principal draftsman of the new Uniform Commercial Code, Llewellyn has insisted upon the re-examination of rules of commercial law in terms of their social functions; Fuller has been a leader in stressing a "purposive" legal philosophy, which links sociological jurisprudence with the natural-law tradition.

It would be wrong to conclude, however, that a natural-law theory is dominant in the United States today. Perhaps the distinguishing characteristic of our present situation, in this regard, is that no theory is dominant and, indeed, no theory is asserted with complete assurance. This has led some critics to say that we lack a legal philosophy altogether; I think it would be more accurate to say that we recognize elements of truth in several legal philosophies.

These various philosophies are interwoven into the historical development of our legal institutions. We cannot talk about legal theory as something apart from that historical development. Not only our law but also our theories of law are a product of our history, a response to our past and to our future. In this sense I believe we are committed not only to the philosophies which I have so far discussed but also to what has been called "historical jurisprudence." Despite the fact that we have had few jurists who belong to what in Europe is called the "historical school," a historical element is nevertheless built into our legal thought by the very nature of our judicial process. In looking for guidance to the decisions of courts in previous cases, including the reasoning of those decisions and the policies which underlie them, our judges continually marshal past experience in order to develop not only the law but also the philosophy of the law. Since the foundations of our law are judge-made, our law teachers and our lawyers cannot help but absorb a large historical ingredient into their thinking.

In contrast to countries whose legal thought is dominated by Thomist, or by Kantian, or by Marxist, or by Austinian, or by Kelsenist theories, America seems to speak about law with different voices at different times and in different contexts. Our philosophy is rationalist, empiricist, idealist, realist, moralist, positivist, individualist, socialist—all at once. But this is not necessarily a defect. We are able, I would suggest, to reconcile a variety of legal theories which appear inconsistent when viewed in the abstract, just because we do not view them in the abstract, but rather see them in the context of the historical development of our legal system—see them, that is, as partial statements of a truth which is never fully revealed but which finds expression, in time, as we continue to build on our past experience.

HAROLD JOSEPH BERMAN was born in 1918 in Hartford, Connecticut. He attended public schools there, and continued his education at Dartmouth College, the London School of Economics, Yale Graduate School (in History), and Yale Law School. After receiving his LL.B., Mr. Berman was Assistant Professor of Law at Stanford University. In 1948 he began teaching at the Harvard Law School, where he is now a Professor. Mr. Berman's articles appear frequently in periodicals, and his numerous books on the law include *The Nature and Functions of Law* (1958), and several dealing with legal questions in the Soviet Union, such as *Justice in Russia* (1950), and *Soviet Law in Action* (1953). Professor Berman lives in Newton, Massachusetts, with his wife and four children.

THE TEXT of this book is set in Linotype ELECTRA, a face designed by W. A. Dwiggins, who was responsible for so much that is good in contemporary book design. Electra cannot be classified as either modern or old-style. It does not echo a particular period or style. Composed, printed and bound by THE COLONIAL PRESS INC., Clinton, Massachusetts. Cover design by S. NEIL FUJITA.

VINTAGE POLITICAL SCIENCE
AND SOCIAL CRITICISM

VINTAGE WORKS OF SCIENCE
AND PSYCHOLOGY

VINTAGE BIOGRAPHY AND AUTOBIOGRAPHY

VINTAGE HISTORY AND CRITICISM
OF LITERATURE, MUSIC, AND ART

A free catalogue of VINTAGE BOOKS will be sent to you at your request. Write to Vintage Books, Inc., 457 Madison Avenue, New York 22, New York.

VINTAGE HISTORY
EUROPEAN

A free catalogue of VINTAGE BOOKS will be sent to you at your request. Write to Vintage Books, Inc., 457 Madison Avenue, New York 22, New York.

VINTAGE HISTORY
AMERICAN

A free catalogue of VINTAGE BOOKS will be sent to you at your request. Write to Vintage Books, Inc., 457 Madison Avenue, New York 22, New York.